D1497029

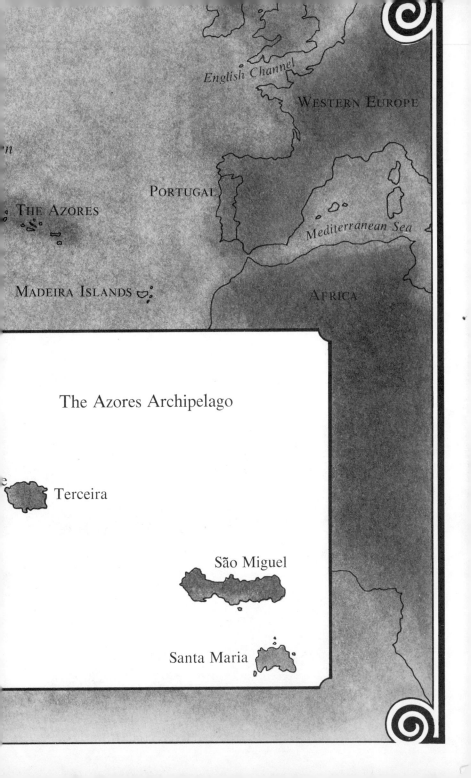

English Channel

WESTERN EUROPE

PORTUGAL

THE AZORES

n

Mediterranean Sea

MADEIRA ISLANDS

AFRICA

The Azores Archipelago

Terceira

São Miguel

Santa Maria

NEVER BACKWARD

Lawrence Oliver

B/OLIVER

OCT 17 1987

NEVER BACKWARD

THE AUTOBIOGRAPHY
OF
LAWRENCE OLIVER
A PORTUGUESE-AMERICAN

Compiled and Dictated

by

Lawrence Oliver

Edited by

Rita Larkin Wolin

SAN DIEGO PUBLIC LIBRARY
HISTORY & WORLD AFFAIRS

© 1972, by Lawrence Oliver, San Diego, California. All rights reserved. Printed by Neyenesch Printers, Inc., 2750 Kettner Boulevard, San Diego, California, United States of America.

To my wife, Mary, a wonderful wife and companion, an excellent mother and homemaker; who has always cooperated with me in everything that I wanted to do; who always placed my wishes and our children's needs above any desires of her own; who has been an integral factor in any measure of success which I have achieved.

To my children, Richard, Doris, and Norman, who also have given me their love and support in all my endeavors. My family has been my inspiration.

CONTENTS

ILLUSTRATIONS

There are three virtues which I have always tried to practice. They are faith, love and determination. They gave me strength when my goals seemed far distant or unobtainable, as often occurred during my lifetime. This book is the true story of a poor, uneducated, immigrant boy, who was guided and assisted by his beliefs until his dreams came true.

Lawrence Oliver

INTRODUCTION

In the middle of the Atlantic Ocean lies a little paradise. "The Garden of the Atlantic," the Azores are called. Three little clusters, totalling nine islands, are situated in a straight line between New York and Gibralter, some 740 miles east of Portugal.

They are especially beautiful when seen from the air or from the ocean. Most of them are high in the center and slope toward the sea. The land is divided into small parcels where corn, wheat, barley, grapes, and other vegetables and fruits are cultivated. The plots are yellow, brown, light or dark green, tan, peach or gold, depending on the maturity of the crop. Vivid flowers and flowering shrubs and trees add to the color. This gives the effect of a gigantic patchwork quilt, lying against a carpet of blue sea.

Portugal's greatest poet, Luis de Camoes, (1524-1580), might well have been describing the Azores when he wrote in his *Lusiads* or Portuguese Sagas of "a shore so flowery and so sweet an air, Venus might build her dearest temple there."

The southwestern group of islands consists of São Miguel, Santa Maria and two spectacular groups of rocks, called the Formigas or Ants, and the Dollabaret. There first were named by the explorer, Pedro Alvares Cabral, who called the second group the Lesser Formigas. Another mariner, Captain P. Dollabarets, in 1788, renamed the smaller formation. Often, in winter storms, these two clusters are enveloped in boiling foam, haze, and fog. Many, many ship tragedies have occurred around these shoals, which are treacherous but beautiful.

The central island group is composed of Faial, Pico, São Jorge, Terceira and Graciosa. The northwestern section contains the islands of Flores and Corvo.

The Azores are further from the mainland than any other group of Atlantic Islands. They stretch from northwest to southwest, rising from more than two and one-half miles deep down on the ocean floor. Peaks extend as high as 6,000 and 7,000 feet above the surface, as in the case of the island of Pico. Scientists believe that the islands and the rock groupings are the pinnacles of an underwater volcanic mountain chain, which extends from Iceland to Antarctica.

Much of the coastline of the islands is composed of lava formations. They all are alike, yet all are different. Pico is known for placid little lakes. Corvo boasts of a large volcanic crater, now a deep lake, from whose surface nine rocks protrude, as though they were replicas of the islands of the Azores.

No one knows for sure how long the Azores were uninhabited or who first visited them. We do know that between about 1427 and 1431 pilots of the king of Portugal, sailing westward at his command, in search of new lands and new routes to the east, came upon what were then barren and untenanted islands. It appeared to them that no human beings ever had lived there or been there before. The Portuguese government claimed them, and settlement was begun in 1432.

The name originated from large flocks of a type of hawk or buzzard which formerly inhabited the islands in profuse fashion. These were called *acor* by the Portuguese.

By the end of the fourteenth century, colonization largely was complete. The people of the Azores are of Portuguese extraction, except for a few Flemings who were allowed to settle in the island of Faial in early colonization times. The first land lieutenant of the island of Faial was a Flemish nobleman, Josse de Hurtere. Although these people soon were absorbed into the Portuguese population, some trace of them remains in the dark-hooded capes of the women and the sturdy Dutch-type windmills.

There are historians who claim that the Azores were visited earlier, that Carthaginian and other ancient coins have been discovered on the islands, principally at Corvo. This claim is not fully accepted as an historical fact. It is true, however, that

Italian and Catalonian maps of the fourteenth century show the islands marked.

In addition to their scenery, the Azores are blessed with a Mediterranean climate. They cover 893 square miles and have a coastline of 320 miles.

Portuguese is considered to be the language closest to ancient Latin, although in it there are some reminders of the invasion of the Moors. This event began around 700 A.D. and was ended when Portugal's independence was recognized by Pope Alexander III, in 1179 A.D. Some 600 Arabic words have been assimilated into Portuguese. Some evidence of the Moors remains in much of the architecture of Portugual and of the islands.

The islanders are Portuguese in every respect, fidelity, religion, customs, philosophy of life—perhaps in many areas of behavior more pure in their habits and traditions. Because of the isolation of their austere but beautiful homeland, the people of the Azores learned early that to exist they must exercise the qualities of self reliance, interdependence, and harmony.

Those who emigrated, carried with them to the New World the instant ability to size up a situation and to seize upon its advantages; automatic assistance to others; and a system of customs and manners which prohibits or eliminates civil or domestic discord.

The Portuguese who came to the United Sates settled in two zones: on the Atlantic coast, from New England to Pennsylvania; and on the Pacific coast, in the state of California.

It is on record, according to the Portuguese historian, Celestino Soares, on page 55 of his book, *California and the Portuguese,* published in Lisbon in 1939, (and recently reprinted) that in the year 1780 men of Faial, Pico, São Jorge, Flores and Corvo, in the Azores, embarked as members of the crews of two hundred whalers which had anchored in the Azores and proceeded later to the United States. He also states that between 1789 and 1815, in Upper California, the Portuguese founded whaling stations at such places as Half Moon Bay, Pescadero,

Monterey, Carmel, San Simon, Point Conception, Portuguese Cove, Portuguese Bend, and San Diego.

The first attention paid by the Portuguese to California as a state in which to settle appears to be the year 1848, according to Soares. He cites *Information and Suggestions Extracted from Official Documents concerning California and her Gold Mines,* written in Portuguese and published at Oporto, in 1849. The booklet, of eighteen pages, suggested that the Portuguese should trade with California and described the advantages of life there. Its emphasis was on trade, rather than colonization, but the pamphlet excited Portuguese curiosity, and the people soon followed. No sooner were they here, than they began to leave their own unique stamp upon the face of California.

There has been no better description made of the Portuguese-Americans than a speech over the N.B.C. radio network in December 1934, by Manuel F. Sylva, a founder and then president of the Cabrillo Civic Club of San Francisco. This Portuguese organization was begun in San Francisco on February 2, 1932, under the name *Dom Nuno Club.* The name was changed in 1934. "The story of the Portuguese in California is the story of California itself, with all its life and color and wealth of incident. The Portuguese have always been a liberty-loving race; their descendants in California are likewise. They are adventurous and courageous, natural pioneers. They are home lovers and home builders. Of a deeply religious nature, they support their church and its needs. Although thrifty, they recognize the good things of life and when acquired, use them with moderation and good judgment. Seldom will their names be found on relief rolls and even less often on the records of our criminal courts.

"In their quiet, unostentatious manner they give their unstinted support to our institutions, whether religious, commercial, educational, or civic. Asking little, giving much, they form an integral and valuable part of our body politic."

R.L.W.

Chapter I

In The Beginning

I don't see how any boy could ever have celebrated his sixteenth birthday in a more memorable fashion than I celebrated mine. I was lurking near a pier in the harbor of São Miguel, in the Azores, looking out on the one hand for the law and on the other for sight of a launch, which, God willing, would smuggle me and several other boys onto a White Star Streamer whose destination was the United States.

I had in my pocket one five dollar gold piece—borrowed. Most of my clothes I wore on my back. I had never been to school. I could neither read nor write, nor could I speak or understand a word of English.

The launch arrived. We jumped in. The men rowed for dear life. Had we been caught, everyone would have been arrested. In a few minutes we met the steamer and boarded her as fast as humanly possible. The ship hoisted anchor. We were on our way to America, on my sixteenth birthday, March 27, 1903!

No one who has not lived in a country as poor as my homeland can ever realize the feelings of joy and hope which filled the hearts of our little group. After we reached the States, I never saw any of those boys again. I hope that their dreams were realized, as mine were. I became a success, so to speak. I made some money. I acquired a wonderful family and many true friends. I have been awarded numerous honors, which I may or may not have deserved. For all these things I am grateful. I feel humble and unworthy of the blessings which God has bestowed upon me.

From my native land to San Diego, California, the distance is several thousand miles. It is, also, a journey from one world into another. No one knows that more clearly than I do.

I was born in Calheta de Nesquim, Island of Pico, Azores. My father was Manuel Lawrence Oliveira and my mother was Maria de Jesus Oliveira.

My native island is about thirty miles long and twelve miles wide. On the west end of the island there is a large volcano 7715 feet high, the highest in the Azores. This volcano is very much alive, but has not erupted for over 125 years.

There are villages clear around the island, all situated near the water. Most of them have their own seaport. Among these are Manhenha, Piedade, Calheta, Ribeiras, Lajes, Silveira, São João, Terra do Pão, São Caetano, São Mateus, Candelaria, Criacão Velha, Madalena, Bandeiras, Santa Luzia, Santo Antonió, São Roque, São Miguel Arcanjo, Prainha, Santo Amaro, and Ribeirinha.

My parents were of modest means. Although the Azores are beautiful, most of the people are poor. Life is hard. There were four children in our family, two boys and two girls. I never knew one of my sisters. She died before I was born, when she was about six years old. Another child, born afterward, was born dead. I was the youngest.

My father had been to the United States twice before I arrived. Eight days later he departed for the States again. I was four years old when he returned.

The first time that my father left—I think that this was before he was married—he was recruited for a whaling ship. These ships came by many times looking through the islands for men for crews. Somewhere on the trip he jumped ship. Whether this was in California or somewhere in the east and he came to California, I don't know. I do know that he worked somewhere in California, in the gold mines. He was in California for three or four years before returning to the Azores. Later he made another trip to the States and returned. After I was born, he left again.

My mother's health was not good after my birth; so I was raised by my godmother, who lived next door. It was her sister, who many years later, in Hanford, California, helped to save my life. Apparently no one expected that I would live to grow up, for I was never given a full name, only the name Lawrence.

The village church at Calheta de Nesquim, Island of Pico, Azores. I was baptized in this church.

When my father returned, I wouldn't have anything to do with him. To me he was a stranger. Some time passed before I accepted him.

Life went at an even pace for about five years after my father's return. During that time he farmed. The farmers helped each other. My sister, Mary, who was three years older than I was, assisted in the house. My brother, nine years my senior, was my father's right arm, helping him with all the chores.

Suddenly two tragic events occurred. We lost my brother and then my mother. My brother, when he was eighteen years old, died from an attack of typhoid fever. From then on I took his place and did his chores. This meant, among other things, taking care of the livestock, two oxen, twelve to fifteen sheep and a calf or two. I milked the cows every day while they were giving milk.

We kept the cows in our pastures, which were five to seven

3

miles from home. When they were five miles from home, I arose as three o'clock in the morning to get there at daybreak. When they were seven miles away, I arose at one o'clock in order to be there by daybreak. I would milk the cows and return home with the milk about noon. I had lunch, rested for an hour, then went to work in the fields for the balance of the afternoon.

I still remember that at one o'clock or three o'clock in the morning everything was dark as pitch. I was fearful, especially when I passed a house where someone had died. When I was a child I was afraid of the dead. (Now, sometimes, I am afraid of the living.)

After leaving the residential district I would go up the roads, or trails, you might call them. They were wooded on both sides. If there were a branch of a tree a little higher than another or moving in the shadows I would imagine that someone stood there, waiting for me. That didn't make me feel good. I would make tracks, with my imagination continuing to work, until I overtook someone going my way for the same purpose as I had.

When I was alone and the birds, flying from tree to tree, made noise, I was positive that something was after me. I would sing at the top of my voice to drown out the frightening sounds. Many times, if no one came along, this would go on until daylight. I was about nine years old, then, just a child, but a child often did a man's work where I came from.

In the Azores, the people own pieces of land that they have inherited. Sometimes the parents from whom they inherited lived far away, on the other side of the district, five, six, or seven miles from where the children lived. Each family, also, had its own pasture for cows, sheep, or whatever else they possessed. This was the way it was with us.

Because of the rough terrain, oxen must be used in the islands. We utilized them to pull the plow, haul a two-wheel cart, and to help grind the wheat and corn. When they got along in years, the people would fatten them up and sell them for meat.

Our methods of farming and harvesting were primitive. When

4

the wheat was ripe, we would cut it by hand and take it to a place which was arranged as a big circle. We would pile the wheat there, then put a big post in the middle with six or eight oxen tied to the post. The one which was closest to the pole would move slowly, but the ones on the outside we chased, to make them move rapidly. The animal's feet would thrash the wheat; so that the grain would separate from the straw. When a good wind would come up, we would take a shovel and toss the material in the air. The wind would blow the chaff away.

When grinding wheat, we used a grinding mill which was composed of two stones about three feet in diameter, with a hole in the top of one. We raised the top one from the bottom one and poured the wheat or corn, whatever we were grinding, through the little hole in the middle. It would go down between the two stones. The oxen provided the power.

We cut wood for fuel and let it dry. Afterward, we would haul it home to use for cooking. We chopped the tender leaves and put them in the barnyard, where the oxen would lie on them and fertilize them. That fertilizer was used for the soil.

When it was time to harvest corn we first broke the tops, the tassles, and put them out to dry. When they were dry, we baled them. We stored them in the barn to feed the stock in the winter. The corn husks were saved for feed for the cattle, and the stalks were dried and baled for the cattle food, also.

We hauled water. There was a fountain close by where we went to get a pot full. Almost every house had a cistern. The water, when it rained, dripped down onto a platform over the cistern, from which the cistern caught the rain. In a dry year, we often went six or eight miles for water. Women carried it in wooden pots on their heads. Often the people cooked with sea water. They still do.

Our home was three rooms and a kitchen. It had a basement, but no upstairs. Where I slept was my bedroom, dining room and everything else. It was a large room and my bed was over in one corner. The mattress was made of corn husks and moss.

5

In some areas the rich people had mattresses made of wool, but we never saw any.

My family home, in Pico. I don't think that we inherited this house. It seems to me that my father bought it when he returned from one of his trips to America. Someone added the cross after I left the islands. A cross means special blessings on the house.

We used coal oil for light, sometimes whale or porpoise oil. Cooking was done in pots set in a three-legged ring under which a fire was built.

Only a year after my brother died, my mother passed away. My sister, Mary, who was only twelve years old, became the woman of the house.

Earlier, Mary had gone to school. My father sent her to a private school to learn to read, not to write. He didn't want her to learn to write. She learned after she came to this country.

My brother had gone to school and my father knew how to read and write but he never sent me to school. There were schools on the island, government schools, but they did me no good. I had no education whatsoever until some time after I arrived in the United States.

Most of the children whom I knew had to work a good deal,

although many of them received some schooling. We had no toys. We invented games to play. During celebrations the people made sky rockets. We would run after the rockets because they were wrapped in twine, which we used to make a line to spin our home-made tops. We'd draw a ring. You would spin your top in the middle of the ring. I would take my top and try to nick yours. Sometimes we put two or three tops in a ring. Someone would take his top and try to knock them all out of the ring at one time.

We played a game similar to tiddly winks. We would use buttons. The losers pulled the buttons off their clothes in order to continue playing, for we played for keeps.

This small boy could have been me. We took this picture on one of our trips to the Azores.

One time my father sent me to check to see if the oxen were in our pasture. On the way I ran into another little boy, and we

7

stopped to play the button game. I forgot all about the stock and didn't tell my father that I hadn't done as he had instructed me. Later a neighbor came to report that the oxen had gotten out of our pasture and were in the neighbor's pasture, chasing his milk cows. What a beating my father gave me! I never forgot it. He impressed on me, then and one other similar time, that I had no time to play, because there was too much work to do.

A big event, when I was a child, occurred when the king of Portugal, Carlos I, visited the island next to ours. He later, in 1908, was assassinated in Lisboa, he and the crown prince, Louis Philippe. Another son, Manuel II, took over, but the government was overthrown in 1910. Since then Portugal has been a republic. The king, when he visited during my boyhood, came to the Azores in a big government ship. My father went to see him. The people had races between their whale boats and fired sky rockets in the king's honor. We had few visitors, though. The bishop came every few years and that was about it, except for the relatives who returned from America.

Three years after my mother's death, my father decided to marry again. My sister and I did not like the idea, yet there was nothing we could do. Things became no easier for us. My stepmother had a godchild, for whom she had cared since he was born. His family had too many other mouths to feed. Although she did not bring him to live with us when she married my father, she was devoted to him. He passed our house on the way to school every day.

Two years passed. The family situation did not improve.

Chapter II

The Land With Gold In The Streets

Early in my life, I don't recall when, my sister and I began to think about going to America. At that time, I had the wrong impression. The Portuguese who had gone there and had returned to visit their parents or to stay, were well dressed, had gold watches and chains, and gold rings. They were glad to show their wealth to us. They did no work. Their relatives waited on them hand and foot, as though they were royalty. This gave me the idea that people lived in America like they were kings and queens. Money just came to them—they picked gold coins off a tree. I wasn't two weeks in the United States before I found out that this wasn't true.

Mary was increasingly unhappy about sharing the home with her stepmother. She was the first of us to go. About two years after our father's second marriage, when she was seventeen, Mary asked my father if he would let her go to America and pay her fare there. He was reluctant at first, but she begged, and he finally agreed. My sister left for New Bedford, Massachusetts, where we had friends. His name was John de Mello. His wife was from Pico. They promised to help Mary get a job.

With Mary gone, I grew more restless than ever. I wanted to go, too. My father heard from Mary. She had a job doing housework. She was happy. I felt that I had to get away from home, to come to the land where the streets were paved with gold. The following year, when I was fifteen, I asked my father to please let me go to the United States and to pay my fare there.

At first he replied no. He was emphatic. He said that I was too young and too lazy, and that in America people had to work hard for what they got. My head was full of foolish dreams, he told me.

I kept at him. Finally, several months later, one day early in February, 1903, he agreed that I could go. He would pay my fare, but there were complications. Because of my age, fifteen, the government would not give me a passport. The government wanted the boys to wait until they were eighteen, then go to serve in the army for two or three years. Maybe after that the officials would give you a passport. There was no guarantee. I didn't want to wait that long, so my father had to pay an agent to smuggle me out of the Azores.

I wasn't doing anything new. These agents were professional smugglers. They operated regular services, for which young men paid a fee in order to get out of the islands. There was always the risk of being caught by the revenue cutter and being brought back to Portugal, in which case one paid a heavy fine. I decided that the risk was worth it. My father went to make the arrangements.

A few days later, he told me that I should get ready. Arrangements had been made. I was to be prepared to leave at any time. I waited, thinking that the time would never come.

On February 11, 1903, my father informed me that I was to leave the next day from Ribeiras, Santa Cruz, which is about three or four miles from Calheta.

I was so excited and so happy that I couldn't sleep that night. I was called at six A.M. and was ready in "no time."

My father and I left for Ribeiras, where I was to take the steamer to go to the island of São Miguel. In all that time, between Calheta and Ribeiras, there was little said between my father and me. He was thinking, and I was thinking. I wondered what America would be like, what kind of work would I do, would I be a success or a failure? Only since I have become a father, can I hazard a guess as to my father's thoughts.

At Ribeiras, we said goodbye. I was on my way, with the five dollar gold piece he had borrowed to give me. My first promise was to pay him back as soon as possible.

My trip took over a month and a half. At the end of it I received a surprise. I saw my father again, much sooner than I had ever expected.

I arrived at São Miguel from Ribeiras two days after leaving my father. There I met the agent and twenty-one other boys, all doing exactly what I was doing. The agent took us nine miles into the country. We traveled at night, so that we would not be observed. The place was called Ribeira Grande. There was an acre of land, on which was situated a big two-story house, with a very high fence around it. The windows had stationary blinds. We could see out, but no one could see in. The rest of the boys spent the whole month and a half at the farmhouse. For me this was not the case.

When we had been there for a week, the agent came to see us. I was the youngest of the boys. Their ages ranged from twenty to thirty-five. The agent asked me if I would like to live with him and be his errand boy. I would be free, not bound to the house. I would be happier. I agreed.

I went to live with the agent, his wife, and his mother-in-law in the city. For a while my fortunes improved, but not for long. Everything was fine as long as he was around. He took me with him to the city, shopping, or to the orchards where there were several varieties of fruits—oranges, apples, bananas, figs, and grapes. I enjoyed these trips, but the good times came to an end.

The agent went to Lisboa, Portugal, on business. He told me to stay with his wife and his mother-in-law, which I did for a short time, but the picture had changed. After he left, I no longer received the same kind treatment as he had given me. Formerly I had been served the same food that the family ate. Now I was living on salted sardines and bread. Once in a while I received a glass of milk. I accepted this treatment for a few days, waiting to see if there would be a change, but no change came.

I decided to leave. That day I started my business career. I made up my mind to run away and to try to go back where the other boys were. I was fearful, though, of walking those nine miles alone. I knew that a stage made the trip every afternoon. They charged something like twenty-five cents. I only had about one-half that amount—money the agent had given me, a few pennies each time that I bought something for him, and he told me to keep the change.

I went to the stage depot to negotiate my fare back to the Ribeira Grande, and told the people at the depot how much money I had. "But it takes twice as much as you have," they explained.

"You can stretch a point and take me for one-half fare. I am a small boy and this is all the money that I have."

"Well, wait until the time of the stage departure." If they did not have a full load, they would take me for half fare. Luck was with me. Late that evening I joined the other boys. They were glad to see me, and I was happy to be back with them.

At the agent's house there were two upset ladies. They had no idea what had happened to me, only that I had disappeared. They didn't learn the truth for over two weeks. When the agent returned from Lisboa, he came to see the boys and found me there.

He told us that he had the plans set, that we would be leaving in approximately two weeks. We would walk the nine miles back to the city. When we arrived, we were not to stick together. We were to scatter, but at a certain time in the afternoon be waiting by the pier. When a launch came, we were to jump in. "Don't waste any time and don't say anything," he cautioned. When the right day came, we did as he told us.

The trip to the United States was unpleasant in many respects. It took seven days. From the moment we left the island of São Miguel, all the way to Boston, Massachusetts, I was seasick every minute of the time. We traveled in steerage. The compartment was crowded with people, many of them as ill as I was. The odor alone was enough to make us all nauseated. When I arrived in America, I had lost several pounds.

It was easy to get into this country in those days. America was a free port. To get in, all you needed was a little money in your pocket, so that the authorities could be sure that you wouldn't be destitute and on relief right away.

We arrived at Boston around 7:00 A.M. Going through customs took most of the day. In the late afternoon we were told by a Portuguese interpreter that he was going to put each of us on the train which would take him to his destination. The boys were going to different points, mostly to California.

My destination was New Bedford, to the same people who had befriended my sister, Mary. Since I could neither read nor write, nor speak a word of English, the interpreter gave me a slip of paper on which my destination was written. There, also, was a note to the policeman at the train station in New Bedford, asking him to guide me, or send me to our friends. The Portuguese interpreter put me on the train at the Boston depot. Soon I was on my way, with my five dollar gold piece in my pocket, and my clothes tied up in a bundle. For the first time, I was riding on a train. I hoped that it was the right train, for there was nothing which I could do to help myself. I had to trust in God and Lady Luck to see that everything would turn out all right.

As so often has been the case in my life, God and luck were with me, and people were kind. At New Bedford, I showed the paper to the policeman at the station. He read it, called a taxi and gave the driver instructions. All the way I worried. How much would the driver charge? How would I know how to pay him? Where I came from people got where they were going by the use of their feet most of the time. That five dollar gold piece was all I had, and I didn't want to change it. Also, I was chilled. The climate in New Bedford, although it was spring, was nothing like that of the Azores. I noticed the difference more, I guess, because I had been sick on the way over on the boat.

Soon the taxi stopped. The driver got out and rang a doorbell. A young lady came to the door. The driver, I found out later, told her that he had a young man in the taxi who couldn't speak English but who had her address. She called her mother. Her mother came out to the taxi and began to talk to me in Portuguese. What a relief! For a minute, after hearing her first words, I thought I had died and gone to heaven.

This was Mrs. de Mello, who greeted me. She paid the taxi fare and brought me into the house. The Mellos gave me dinner and put me up for the night. Once I was in the house, I heard some surprising news. My father and stepmother had arrived in New Bedford that morning! I had no idea that he was thinking of coming to America, but he must have had the idea in his mind for some time. He was not well, and to make a living in Portugal was hard, for there was much heavy physical labor. Besides, my sister and I were here.

The next morning we had a family reunion. My sister, also, was present. My father was concerned because I was so long on the way to America. "Where have you been?" he asked. "I thought you must have been picked up by the revenue cutter and taken back to Portugal."

He had been so sure that something had happened to me that he had arranged with a friend to sell a piece of property in the Azores in order to get me free. How could I let him know how long I had been forced to wait in São Miguel for the steamer to take me to America, I asked him. I could neither read nor write.

Chapter III

Life In New Bedford And Chico

It did not take me long to discover that America was a good deal different from what I had pictured my my mind. I soon learned that the streets were not paved with gold. Instead, I discovered that, in one instance at least, they were paved with big rocks.

Our friends found me a job working on a farm at five dollars a month, plus room and board. The farmer was Portuguese, from the island of Flores. I took care of two horses, milked two cows, cleaned the barn, watered and fed the stock and worked in the fields until four in the afternoon. Then I stopped to do the chores. One morning, however, things changed.

I got up as usual and did my chores, then had breakfast. Afterwards the boss said, "Come with me." He took me to the shed and picked up a sledge hammer. We went to the middle of the field, where there was a big pile of rocks. He broke a few and then gave me the hammer, telling me to break the big ones to a certain size for the crusher. He said I should come to the house for lunch at noon and then return to break rocks until four o'clock, when I was to do the chores.

I was a very small boy for my age. All morning I swung that hammer, as he had told me to do. At noon I dragged myself to lunch. By the time four o'clock came, my hands were blistered and sore. I had a hard time milking the cows. When I went to dinner, I sat at the table and I could not eat.

I went to bed and cried all that night. I was ashamed, for I do not often cry. I never cried when my father beat me—never in his presence. I burst into tears afterward, sometimes, remembering my mother. Only two times since being in the United States, have I cried.

The next morning I went to do the chores the best way that I could, but I moved with great difficulty. After breakfast the farmer told me to go out in the field to break more rocks. I knew I couldn't handle that hammer for another day. I handed it back to him. "You go break them yourself. You are bigger than I am. I didn't come to America to break rocks for my living."

I left that farm, not even waiting for the two dollars and fifty cents I had coming for my first two weeks of work. With my clothes tied up into the bundle, I started walking down the road, heading toward New Bedford, which was about eight miles away.

I couldn't speak any English to ask for help, but I wasn't too concerned. I had it in my mind to find a certain five and dime store, in the downtown area. It had a peanut roasting machine which whistled as it roasted peanuts. That caught my eye when I first came to New Bedford and it stuck in my mind. I had never seen anything of the sort before. It was my landmark, for I knew that my sister worked in a house nearby.

Once in the city, I walked up and down the streets until I spotted the store. From there I walked some more until I located my sister.

After I told her what had happened, she found a place for me to stay that night. The next morning she saw to it that I was taken to where my father and stepmother were staying; so I could tell them my story. They were with friends from Portugal who owned a farm outside the city.

Did I ever get a bawling out from my father! He told me that I was lazy and didn't want to work, and that I would never amount to anything! When I tried to explain, he wouldn't listen. I still don't know why he would say that I was lazy and didn't want to work. I had been doing a man's work since I was nine years old.

I stayed with my father and stepmother that night. He wasn't very happy with me at all. The next morning I heard that the lady with whom we were staying was going into town that day. She made cheese. Two or three times a week she went into the city to sell it. I inquired if I could go with her, explaining that I wanted to look up a friend of mine who worked in a cotton mill. I wanted to ask him if he could help me get a job. She was glad to take me along. We hitched up the horse and buggy and drove into town.

I went to the boarding house where my friend was living, to wait for him to come home that evening. He was a former neighbor of mine, from the old country. We had grown up together. His name was José Vitorino Machado. That night I asked him about getting me a job in the mill. He was glad to try to help me. The landlady permitted me to stay overnight and told me that if I got a job I could have board and room privileges there.

When my friend came home the next night, he had a job for me at three dollars and fifty cents per week. My room and board, including laundry, would cost me two dollars and fifty cents a week. The next day I went to work, sweeping floors in a cotton mill. In about three months I was promoted to being a cleaner, but my pay stayed the same for a year.

I worked hard while there. Also, I watched the rest of the workers doing their jobs. Whenever I could, I helped them, with the idea in my mind of learning the work, getting promotions, and more money. I was learning that in America gold wasn't being found in the streets, but that if I worked hard, I could achieve more than I ever could dream of acquiring in the Azores.

In a year I saved thirty dollars. I went to one show, a vaudeville show, during that time. We sat way up in the "peanut gallery." It cost me ten cents and I loved it. I have always liked music. When I got home, however, and told the boardmaster what I had done, I got a bawling out. I was squandering my money, the people told me.

One thing that I didn't like about my situation during that year was that I had no opportunity to learn any English. I worked with Portuguese people and lived with Portuguese people all during that time. Even my boss was Portuguese.

I remember, also, that I went through many cold days in New Bedford. The climate was not like Pico, and I was forced to buy warm clothes for the winter months. That was a big adjustment.

At that time, and for the first couple of years that I was in the United States, my main thought was to make something of myself—to get a good job and make some money, to accomplish something. Later, my feelings began to change. My big dream became to have a business of my own. Another goal I had was that if I married and had a family, to be able to give my children a good education. These two things were my biggest ambitions. I never was ambitious to get rich. I am not rich today. I wanted to be able to support my family and to have money for its needs. Also, I wanted to be able to do something for all the people who had been kind and helpful to me. One thing that I have always regretted is that by the time I was in a position to repay some of the people who had been good to me, it was too late. They were gone.

My father and stepmother had not stayed long in New Bedford. He had a friend from the old country, Joe Miller, he was my sister's godfather by proxy, who wrote to my father in New Bedford, advising him to come to the little coastal town of San Diego. There it would be easier to find work. Joe Miller had been in San Diego for some time. He later became my business partner and still later my father-in-law. He was one of the finest men whom I have ever known.

About a year after I arrived in the States, my father wrote from San Diego for my sister and me to come to California. He was working in a wholesale fish house. He wanted Mary to come to San Diego, and for me to go to a place called Chico, where I had an uncle named John and an aunt named Francesca. Uncle John was a bachelor and had no place for me, but Francesca was married to John P. Valine, who had lost his wife and had been left with six children, four of them still of school age. They were relatives on my father's side.

My fare cost more than the thirty dollars that I had saved; so my sister paid the rest. We came to California by train. My uncle John met me at Sacramento and took me up to Chico, north of Sacramento, to my aunt and her husband. He was another wonderful man. I will never forget him. He was a father to me, and always treated me as though I were one of his own children. He was engaged in agricultural farming and fruit growing.

The first thing he told me was, "You are going to work for me in the summer. I will pay you one dollar a day, room, board and laundry."

This is the farm near Chico, where I lived and worked when I came to California.

That sounded fine—but what he said next didn't set well with me. "In the winter you will have to go to school. You will do some chores in the morning and evening. It won't cost you anything to go to school. You can ride with my children."

I was eighteen years old! To go to school and to be in the first grade with six-year-old children seemed too much to take. "No," I argued, "I want to work and make money." After all, I hadn't repaid my father the loan for my fare to the States, I reminded him.

He was insistent, however, that I go to school, so off I rode in a two-wheel cart crowded with children. If I cried easily I would have cried—I was that embarrassed.

The name of that school was Salem. My uncle's children were younger than I was but were much more advanced. They had a longer day than I had. This turned out to be a great advantage for me because the first grade teacher was a wonderful woman and a great teacher. I wish that I could remember her name. When the first grade would let out, she would say to me, "Now, Lawrence, you stay after school until the other children are ready to go home." She would take me to the blackboard and work with me for an hour or more on spelling, reading, writing, and arithmetic. In one year she put me through the first, second and third grades. The rest of my education I received later in San Diego.

It was at that time that I was going to school in Chico that my name was changed from Oliveira to Oliver. The teacher said that "Oliveira is too long. You must spell it out every time that you give someone your name." I became Lawrence Oliver and have remained that way. I kept the name when I came to San Diego and later when I went into business for myself. Most Portuguese people who came to San Diego, or other places for that matter, at that time, and went into business where they dealt with the Americans, changed their names to common English names. This is what the Americans preferred. When I obtained my citizenship, in 1918, I kept the name Oliver. My children often have asked me, "Dad, why didn't you change it back to Oliveira?" I didn't and it is too late now.

Salem School, in Chico, California, where I first went to school.

When school let out that first year that I lived with my uncle and aunt, I went to work for him full time. When I finished, it still was too early to go back to school. A young friend asked me to go with him to Yreka, far up in northern California, near the border. There was plenty of work there, harvesting, and we would get a dollar and a half per day, plus board. We could sleep in the hayloft.

Meanwhile, my father had written, asking me to come to San Diego to live. I figured that if I could work that one more month, I would have enough money to take care of all my moving expenses.

We went to Yreka and then on to the Siskiyou Mountains. In order to save expenses on transportation, we decided to each buy a bicycle and to travel that way back to Chico. We paid ten dollars apiece for two second-hand bicycles and started out.

They turned out to be a bad bargain. The first day of traveling was fine, but on the second day the chain on my bicycle broke. From then on, I walked and pushed the bicycle for a distance of almost one hundred miles. It took us a week to make the trip of approximately one hundred and fifty miles back to Chico. This was in the fall of 1906.

I gathered my possessions, said goodbye to my relatives, and started for San Diego, traveling by train to San Francisco and then on by boat.

Chapter IV

First Days In San Diego

In coming to San Diego, I was following a Portuguese trend. The little town, with its bay and its mild climate, appealed to my people. Although the history books tell us that the first Portuguese to come to San Diego was João Rodrigues Cabrilho, in 1542, not many Portuguese seem to have come to this part of the country for more than three hundred years after that time.

My wife, Mary, is the historian in our family. She, at one time, researched the history of the Portuguese of San Diego. According to what she learned, the first Portuguese settled here in 1876, in Point Loma, across the bay from San Diego. They were Manuel and Rosalina Madruga. They were followed by such men as Manuel Cabral; Frank Goulart; Manuel S. Soares; John Monise; Joe and Manuel Monteiro; Manuel, John and Mattias Silveira Soares (three brothers); Antonio Medeiros Monise and his brother; Jose Viera Soares; Manuel S. Goulart; Francisco Goulart; and Joe Miller, who, as I indicated before, became my father-in-law. Joe Miller's real name was Silva. These men were from the Island of Pico, in the Azores. Their group landed on the east coast first and settled in Gloucester, Massachusetts. Later some of them went to Half Moon Bay and the San Francisco Bay area. Eventually some came to San Diego.

Since they were fishermen, they settled near the water. Their living was to be made from the sea. They used small sailboats, twenty-six to twenty-eight feet long. The men depended on the wind to take them to the fishing banks. When the wind failed, they rowed.

No women came with them. Once they were settled, however, they sent for their wives and sweethearts. They established homes in La Playa and Roseville, two villages now part of Point Loma, and began raising their families. The fifth generations of some of those families still live in Point Loma.

After bringing in their hauls of fish, the Portuguese fishermen unloaded them on piers and into sheds, which they had built. There the fish were split, salted and placed in tanks for shipping. I remember these piers. They were long and narrow, with the sheds built beside them. Sidewheel steamers plied the waters between San Diego and San Francisco in those days. They were similar to the boats used on the Mississippi River. The steamers were the chief source of transportation in and out of San Diego for many years, for both people and goods. On their return trips from taking the fish and other items to be sold elsewhere, they brought grocery supplies, such as flour, sugar, salt, lard, beans, and cash, if there was any left.

The families raised their own vegetables and fruits. They carried wood from the hills and the beaches for cooking and heating. Water, brought in barrels from across the bay, was doled out in a careful fashion. This was a hard life, but the fishermen were happy. They assisted each other in their work and turned to each other for entertainment and companionship.

The men enjoyed playing cards—the Portuguese love to play cards—and during the evenings they amused themselves in this manner while their wives sewed or baked. On special occasions there was a *Chamarita,* a Portuguese dance.

The first primary school was in Roseville. The first masses were said in the same building on Scott and Cannon Streets until Saint Agnes Church was built. The people were very religious. The patron saint of the fishermen is *Nossa Senhora da Boa Viagem,* Our Lady of Good Voyages.

There was no transportation. Everyone walked. Since the streets were not paved, dust often was ankle-deep.

The Madruga family, which had four sons, moved across the bay to San Diego in order to give their sons a higher education. Manuel Madruga, Senior entered the wholesale fish business,

Before the turn of the century, my wife's father started a ship's chandlery, at the foot of Market Street. This was after he moved from Point Loma to San Diego. It was called "Miller and Company." We can't identify any of the people in the picture. It is possible that the man who is fourth from the left of the group standing in front of the store is Joe Miller, but we are not sure. This picture is a sad momento of the fire which destroyed my wife's family home and killed her young brother. It was one of the few items salvaged. The scorch marks around the edges are visible.

25

and Joe Miller entered the ship chandlery trade. Joe and Manuel Mahans already were in business. They are considered the first Portuguese to live in the city of San Diego.

Mr. and Mrs. Madruga, Senior were a very prosperous and respected couple. My wife still remembers visiting in their lovely home with the beautiful furnishings. Mary always thought that Mrs. Madruga was a fascinating person—a true Portuguese lady. She died at the age of 105 years. Their son, Manuel, who lived most of his life in San Diego, was one of the best designers and boat builders in southern California. He designed and built many tuna clippers. He is my wife's godfather.

Manuel Madruga worked for Manuel Goulart as an apprentice boat builder. Goulart built boats on Atlantic Street, which is now Pacific Highway, between Broadway and E Streets.

I remember the boat, the *Butcher Boy,* owned by the Hardy family. They had a meat packing plant out near Mission Bay and a market called the Bay City Market, on Fifth and G Streets. They, also, owned the San Diego Market and several others and were agents for Cudahy Packing Company. Charlie Hardy was an important man in politics here. The *Butcher Boy* traded with the fishermen.

Although it was Manuel Goulart's firm which contracted to built the boat, it was Mary's godfather, Manuel Madruga, who did the work. As I said, he was the chief designer of boats in the tuna fleet here up until 1955. The last firm he worked for was Campbell Machine Company.

Mary's uncle, Joe Lawrence, was the first Portuguese to go into the fresh fish business here, Manuel Soares went in with him in 1905.

People have told me that the Chinese were here as early as 1869, and that they were San Diego's first commercial fishermen. They fished from junks and brought their catches into the local markets. They salted, dried, and sometimes even iced fish. Their exports went north to San Francisco, and west to the Orient and the Hawaiian Islands.

These Chinese had fishing camps with huge drying racks, south of the little community of Roseville. Roseville was laid out by a man named Louie Rose, in 1870. He was quite active here in San Diego. He wanted a transcontinental railroad to come to San Diego and to terminate in Point Loma, around Ballast Point, as I understand the idea. For many years there was a monument to him right up at the head of Rose Canyon, where the University of California at San Diego now is situated.

Many of the Chinese lived in the area of a wharf, which was at the foot of H Street, west of what is now Pacific Highway. A man by the name of Stephen S. Culver built that wharf in the 1850s.

The Chinese lost most of their fishing business when the state of California passed a very harsh law against them. It restricted immigration into the States, and forbade them to own property. They couldn't even fish because if they went outside the three mile limit, they couldn't come back into the States. Those Chinese used to fish, oh, my golly, way down off the Cedros Islands, 300 or more miles from here. They were good fishermen. They were the first ones, as I understand it, to fish for abalone and had quite a business established.

By the time I arrived in San Diego though, almost all of the Chinese junks were gone. The Portuguese and the Italians dominated the fishing industry. A little later, the Japanese began to make an appearance and were active until World War II began.

My first home in San Diego was with my father and step-mother on Columbia Street, between Ash and Beech. My sister, Mary, was living out and doing day work.

A distant relative, Joe Lawrence, also my wife's uncle, offered me both a job in his fish market and a chance to go to school. Joe Lawrence, you remember, was the first Portuguese to go into the fresh fish business here.

I started to work for him at one dollar a day. I got up early in the morning, picked up two or three boxes of fish of different kinds and visited all of the restaurants to supply their needs for the day. I carried a basket and a spring-hanging scale. It was composed of a little box with a face similar to that of a clock and it had numbers as a clock has. The scale worked on a spring, with hooks on the bottom and on the top. I grabbed it by the hook on the top, then hooked the bottom to the basket, saw the weight of the basket and its contents, then subtracted the weight of the basket.

The early morning hours, before eight, I spend going around with a horse and wagon. I took orders, filled them, collected the money or rendered a bill. By eight o'clock, I was at the market. I then took shipments of fish to the American Railway

The fifth and sixth grades of the Middletown School, when I attended it, in 1907. The principal, Pete Ross, is standing in the rear. My fifth grade teacher, Mrs. Coffeen, also is standing in the rear. I am at the end of the second row from the right. The girl three seats in front of me was named Eldora. The boy at the head of my row was the son of Mrs. Price, who taught at Washington School.

Express. The market had customers in such Southern California towns as Riverside, San Bernardino, Colton, Pomona, Los Angeles, and San Fernando. The butchers in those towns sold fish at least twice a week; so we shipped fresh fish to them twice a week. We packed it in ice and sent it on the morning train. We shipped to Arizona, San Francisco, and the rest of the country.

After I completed these jobs, I would go home to get ready for school. I was in attendance at the Middletown School from 9:00 A.M. to 2:30 or 3:00 P.M. The school address was 1825 State Street. It was built around 1888. Pete Ross was the principal and the teachers I had were a Mrs. Rose in the fourth, Mrs. Coffeen, (I don't think I have her name spelled correctly) in the fifth grade, and Miss Evans in the sixth grade. In two semesters I managed to get through the sixth grade. I was nineteen years old, twice the age of most of my classmates.

After school I would go home, change clothes again and go back to the fish market until the work for the day was completed. There was no regular quitting time in those days. Saturdays, and sometimes on Sundays, we would work all day; yet I was happy, and I was grateful that I had a job and a chance for some more education. This all ended, though, at the end of my second semester, because my employer, Joe Lawrence, ran into some problems.

The group of fishermen who had worked for him decided that they wanted to go into business for themselves. He told them that if they were going to do that he would have no need for the market and for his equipment. He sold it to them. They formed a partnership of eleven men. Not one of them knew anything about running a business; so they hired a young man to keep the books and to operate the firm. I stayed on with them. I cleaned fish, packed fish, shipped fish, as I had done before; however, I didn't go around with the wagon anymore.

When school began that fall, and I asked them about going back, they informed me that I either should quit the schooling or quit the business. I had no choice. I had to support myself.

29

I was paying board and room to my father and stepmother, ten dollars a month. They did not give me any help.

Another person in our home at that time was her godchild, who was living with them and going to school. He did not work. He was about five years younger than I was. They brought him over soon after they came to the States. He later worked for Mary's uncle in Oakland, if I remember correctly. After that, he had a retail fish market in Hayward, outside of Oakland. He passed away a few years ago. We were friendly.

I was disappointed over being forced to abandon my education. My lack of formal schooling is something which I have always regretted. Soon other worries made me forget my disappointment, though. The business didn't make any progress. In fact, it was going into a decline.

I could see some things that were wrong; so I made a few suggestions, but the new manager didn't appreciate my advice. He informed me that if I didn't like the manner in which he was operating the business, I could quit. I did. I couldn't see any future for me in a place which was going downhill. I, also, didn't see any future for the firm, due to the way it was being run.

I was out for three or four days when some of the owners came to me and talked about going back to work. I told them that I didn't see any point in going back because I would get fired again. I didn't think that the business was being run right and couldn't help saying so. They offered me a chance to go into partnership with them, a one-twelfth interest in the business. I could pay in so much a month. I then, supposedly, would have some say about the policies.

I decided to give the proposition a try. I accepted their offer and went back to work. As I was now a part owner, and saw more and more things that I didn't like—some were inefficient and some dishonest—I called the members of the board of directors together and told them what I had seen and found. They didn't believe me. They implied that I wanted the manager's job, but that was far from my mind. In the first place, I didn't know how to keep books. I wanted to work for a firm that had some future. I wanted to make some money. I waited a little longer. When the directors didn't make any moves toward improvement, I asked for my fifty dollar investment to be returned, and I left. That ended my fishing industry career for a while.

Chapter V

Speaking Of Lobsters

There were two other important developments in my life during this same period. The first occurred when my father decided to move to Riverside, inland from Los Angeles and about one hundred miles from here. He asked me to go along, but I decided against it.

I saw the chance to break away, to be on my own. I had never been close either to my father or my stepmother. My father was a serious man. His word was law. I never really worked with him, even in the old country, except on rare occasions. We never talked, the way a boy often talks to his father. After my mother died, I always felt alone.

When my father left San Diego, I went to live with another Portuguese family. As things turned out, I married one of their daughters. The man's name was Joe Miller, the friend from the Azores who had told my father to come to San Diego. The Millers lived on what is now Pacific Highway, at Ash Street. They had eight children, but they only raised four of them. Among them, when I moved in, was one little girl about eight years old. She had brown hair and big brown eyes. She was a nice kid. Her name was Mary. She was born on April 24, 1899, in Middletown. I didn't pay much attention to her, though. We didn't have anything in common. I was twenty years old. We never dreamed, her father and I, that he would become my father-in-law. I never thought that she paid much attention to me, either, but Mary, years later, when I started putting this book together, told me that she always thought that I was "it." She always thought that there was something special about me. That was news to me. I figured that it was my uniform, when I went off "to fight Pancho

Villa," just before World War I began, that got to her.

Mary's family rented that house. It was a good sized place. The lot was a block long and half a block wide. They had a cow, raised chickens and rabbits, and had a vegetable garden. The bay, at that time, was across the street from the house. Nearby, there was a little beach and a pool called Naylor Swimming Tank. The tank was filled with salt water from the bay. This was approximately at the foot of Hawthorne Street.

The other place to swim at that time was across the street from the old Santa Fe Depot (which later was torn down for the 1915 exposition here). It was called Los Baños Bathhouse. This bathhouse was built by Elisha S. Babcock, one of the men who developed Coronado and built the Hotel del Coronado.

Joe Miller, my father-in-law, for many years owned a saloon called Snug Harbor. It was at the corner of Atlantic Avenue and G Street. In this picture Joe is behind the bar, with Frank Lawrence, my wife's uncle, at the right. Frank was a partner in the bar for many years. I am not sure whether he was a partner at the time that this picture was taken.

Joe Miller, my wife's father, had several types of business during his lifetime. He had a ship chandlery, a saloon, a fishmarket, and I don't remember what all else he was into. My wife's moth-

Mary and her brother, Joe Miller, when they had their first communion.

35

er's name was *Emerenciana,* a very old Portuguese name.

My wife is the best one to describe what her family was like. "Our home, when I was a child, was a very happy place. Every Sunday my mother's family congregated at the house. My mother came from a big family. She had nine brothers and sisters living in the area. My father's relatives were in Massachusetts. They did not have the opportunity to visit with him until they all were elderly. My mother's family, though, all had children and grandchildren here.

This was one of Mary's classrooms, when she was in attendance at Washington School. Mary is in the fourth row from the left and to the left of the teacher. She is wearing big bows on either side of her head. When I attended this school, it was called Middletown. For some reason, its name was changed to Washington. The old school was torn down in 1914 and a new Washington School was built. It was torn down a few years ago, for a freeway.

"We enjoyed each other's company. In the evenings, or on Sunday afternoon, the men would play cards. My mother and father would have a conference in the kitchen when the family members appeared. That was a huge kitchen. After the conference, my father would disappear. Soon he'd be back, loaded down with groceries. My mother would fix a dinner. After the meal, the men would settle down to play cards. My father loved to play cards. When he was winning, he was very happy. He would say to the loser, 'Why don't you put your hat on the chair and go take a walk?'

"When he lost it was a different story. He wasn't happy at all. One of the card games they loved to play at the house was a game called *Sueca*.

"My father loved music. He loved to dance. He always was whistling and singing, making jokes. My mother never danced a step in her life. She detested card games and never played them; yet we went to all the dances, and we had card games by the bushel. My mother kept busy during the games. She made doughnuts and popcorn, cakes and sweetbreads, and, always, pots and pots of coffee. My father was an outgoing person. My mother was quiet and serious and dependable. She had a strength that you didn't see on the surface. My mother and father were so different; yet each one let the other one be what he was.

"I had so many cousins—there was never any loneliness in our family. We always had each other to turn to. Years later, when I married Lawrence and scarcely saw him because he was working long hours, I never was despondent, or lonely, or blue.

After the fire which destroyed her family home, in 1911, the Millers moved out of the Middletown School district, and Mary began attending the Franklin School. Here Mary is in the garden which the children had as a school project. She is in the back row, the third pupil from the left, with the big white bows in her hair.

I had my family. I picked up the kids and went to my folks, or some cousins, or they came to see me. It was a blessing to have them nearby."

I enjoyed living with the Millers. I had never experienced much family life. If my mother had lived, things might have been different—who knows?

I stayed with the Millers for a couple of years or more—until the night that they had the fire. That was in 1911. I wasn't at the house that evening. I was at school, studying to be a citizen. When I came home, I discovered that everything was gone— burned up—and one of Mary's little brothers, Manuel, was dead.

My wife remembers that her mother and all the children were at home that evening. "My father had gone to sea because of his health. The doctors felt that he needed more air and sunlight; so he went on a fishing voyage.

"He owned his saloon at that time. My uncle, Frank Lawrence, Joe Lawrence's brother, was in charge. He was a partner. My mother took his meals to him at the saloon. That evening, after putting potatoes to cook to make the yeast for bread, she fixed Frank's dinner, then called her sister to come to stay with us while she went to the saloon.

"My younger sister was asleep. She was a child of about six. My youngest brother was about three years old. We were playing together, we children. My aunt came to the door. At that same moment the kitchen turned into one big blaze.

"The conclusion that we came to later was that the little boy, my little brother who died in the fire, (he was about eight years old) was in the kitchen alone. He turned on the other burner of our old gasoline stove and the gasoline took fire.

"My aunt rushed us out of the house. She remembered that my sister was missing and went back for her. From this her arms were burned a little, and so was her face. My sister, also, had some minor burns.

"My mother came dashing home. The fire trucks had come. She looked us over and discovered that my brother was missing.

With everyone yelling at her to stop, she ran back into the old frame house. By that time, it was an inferno. Since my brother was a shy little boy, my mother thought that he might be frightened and hiding somewhere in the house. She rushed into a bedroom to look for him, but she couldn't find him. She was trapped. Everything around her was on fire. She opened the bedroom window to climb out but couldn't make it by herself; so she called and called, until the firemen came and dragged her through the window.

"Still my brother was missing. My mother was frantic. She kept wanting to go back in the house to look for him, but the people held her back and told her, 'We saw him. He's all right.' Finally she was calm.

"We had recently put in indoor plumbing facilities on our back porch. It was quite the thing. Most people had outhouses. This is where they found the child's body after the fire was out, and the smoke had cleared away. He went there to hide after starting the fire, and he was afraid to come out.

"All we salvaged from that fire was a sewing machine and a shawl. I was about ten years old then, but I still remember the awful empty feeling."

I came home that night and discovered that all of my belongings were gone—everything except the clothes on my back. My savings, thirty dollars, also were gone. It was nothing compared to what the Millers had lost, but I did have some problems. I needed clothes and had very little money. That situation involved me in a disagreement with one of San Diego's leading clothing store owners.

Since leaving the fish market, I had worked for two different bakeries. My first job was at a firm called Southern California Baking Company, on Fourteenth Street, at C. It was run by two German men. I heard that there might be an opening there; so I went to apply. My job consisted of taking a horse and wagon, loaded up with French bread, and making the rounds every morning.

All that I ever delivered from that bakery was French bread. I started out with the wagon and a basket and would go from door to door, asking how many loaves of bread each person wanted. There were two of us on the route. We'd collect the money, or put it on the charge, and go on. The bakery baked white bread, milk bread, rye bread, pumpernickel and other kinds. I worked at this job for about eight months and learned to speak a few words of German.

I left Southern California Baking Company to go to work for Excel Baking Company. It was on Fifth and E. The job paid a little more money. There was a candy store on one side and a delicatessen on the other. The bakery was in the back. A men's clothing firm, called Lion, was right across the street.

The store baked bread both for the delicatessen and for delivery. I would load up the wagon with all kinds of bread, pies and cakes, cookies, and whatever the bakery had available that day. I delivered from door to door.

We had regular customers to whom we delivered all the time. In addition, we had a big bell in the wagon, and we rang the bell as we went up and down the streets. If someone wanted something or to see what we had, he came to the front door. If no one appeared we moved on.

At some places we went to the back to ask what they wanted. We served and collected or charged, then left. Late in the evening we'd go back to the bakery, unload what remained, take the horses to the stable, feed them and go home. I was making between twelve-fifty and fifteen dollars a week at that time.

After the fire, I needed a suit of clothes. I didn't have the money to pay cash, so I went across the street to Mr. Foxx, who was the owner of the Lion Clothing Store and asked him to sell me a suit of clothes on time. I offered to pay him ten or fifteen dollars down—a week's wages—and the balance on time. I explained what had happened to me and where I worked—right across the street. He could look out his window and see me.

He said he would think it over. I was to come back to con-

I had a full head of hair when this picture was taken, around 1910. This was before my typhoid fever attack.

clude the deal and to make my selection. I went to work. When I returned that evening, my coworkers came to me and said, "Did you go across the street to try to buy a suit of clothes on time?"

"Yes."

"Well, he was over here investigating, wanting to know what kind of a fellow you were, whether you were honest and paid your bills on time. We gave you a good recommendation."

I didn't say anything, but I was burned. It seemed to me that he had gone behind my back. If he had wanted references, he could have asked me for them. When I was finished with the work for the day, I went across the street and told Mr. Foxx, "I don't want your suit."

He looked surprised. "Why?"

"You don't trust me. I don't trust you." I left.

I didn't buy anything from Lion Clothing Store for a long time—many, many years. By then, it was moved to Broadway and Sixth.

I was driving the horse and wagon for American Railway Express when this picture was taken. Los Baños Bathhouse is in the background.

This is another view of my American Railway Express days. I don't recall the name of the fellow next to me, holding the reins.

I always kept looking for ways in which to improve my working conditions. After a year with Excel Bakery, I applied for a position with the American Railway Express. On my route I had talked to different people about jobs. I heard of a vacancy there and went to apply for it, figuring that it would be a place to advance, but I was wrong. I delivered parcels. We employees worked on Sundays, and holidays, New Year's, and all. We had one day off a week, but never a Sunday. (I think that's why someone wrote the song, "Never on Sunday.") I didn't like this. The pay was fifty dollars a month, though; so I didn't quit. I kept looking around until something better turned up.

Many times I delivered to a firm called Western Metal Supply Company, on Seventh and L Streets. I heard that it was a good place to work. The employees didn't work Saturday afternoons, or Sundays, or holidays, and there were chances for promotion. One day I applied for a job with them. I talked to the general manager, Paul Rayburn, Senior. He said he would see what he could do for me.

The next day I made a delivery there, and Mr. Rayburn said, "Mr. McKenzie, the owner, wants to see you. I think he is going to offer you a job." (This was Bernard W. McKenzie, the president of the firm.)

When I went to see Mr. McKenzie, he offered me a job driving a horse and wagon. I delivered hardware, plumbing supplies, bathtubs, pipe, sheet metal, and so on. About six months later the company bought a delivery truck, and I was transferred from the wagon to the truck. That was a big time! At least that was what I thought at first. This truck was the fifth one in San Diego. Charlie Hardy, who had the meat packing plant, had two Reliances, and the mayor of San Diego, W. Adam, had two Packards, which made runs between San Diego and Julian. The truck I drove was a Randolf, a one-ton flat rack truck, chain drive, (which means that a chain turns the axle) and solid tires. There was no cab. The engine was underneath the seat and there was no dashboard. The only thing in front of me was the radiator. The truck had two horizontal cylinders.

I took driving lessons from the man who sold us the truck. He was a mechanic. He took me out half a dozen times.

The Randolf Truck

The truck was something new to me—and to most of the town. When I drove by, dogs would bark, and horses would whinney, and all the kids would come running out. The streets weren't paved. They weren't in the shape they are now, with the city keeping them up. You kept your own street up, free from rocks and ruts, as much as you could.

Since the tires were solid rubber, when it rained that truck would skid around as though the streets were greased. Often I found myself stuck, in a downpour. Sometimes I dug myself out with a shovel or got a plank to put underneath the truck. I jacked up the wheel and shoved the plank under it. I used gravel, or sand, or anything that the wheel might grab. When all this failed —and this was often—I resorted to being pulled out by a horse and wagon. At these times, I had the feeling that I hadn't progressed much.

People didn't know much about cars in those days. They expected too much of the truck. We delivered everywhere, regardless of the condition of the streets. This was about the period of 1910-1912, when Loma Portal and San Diego were beginning to build up. I delivered many pipes, and bathtubs, and toilets to Loma Portal over bumpy trails—that's all they were—full of ruts and holes.

A year later, I was promoted to the packing and shipping room. I made seventy-five dollars a month, with no work on Saturday afternoons, Sundays, or holidays—and no digging a truck out of the mud. Soon after that I was made shipping clerk, at eighty-five dollars a month. I was happy. I saw myself making progress. I suppose that I could have continued with Western Metal indefinitely and could have had a future with them, but that wasn't to be.

That year Western Metal gave me a two-week vacation. I went to San Francisco to see some of my relatives. On my return, I came through the San Joaquin Valley, stopping at Hanford to visit my godmother's sister, Mrs. Fernandes, who had been my neighbor in the Azores. She, also, helped to care for me when I was a baby. When I arrived in Hanford I was ill, too ill to eat. The next morning the family called the doctor. He diagnosed typhoid fever. He said that I must go to the hospital. There was only one hospital in town, the Ana Dorn Sanitarium. I was there for almost six months.

After the fever left me, I had a hemorrhaging of the intestines. I almost died. The doctor gave up. He didn't come to see me for over a week. The good Lord, though, was on my side, and I had a wonderful nurse. She asked the superintendent if she could put a cot in my room, in order that she could care for me at night. That's what she did. She was the one, with the help of God, who pulled me through.

When I left the hospital, I weighed eighty pounds. The nurse picked me up in her arms and took me in a horse-drawn buggy to the home of Mrs. Fernandes. They laid me in bed, for I was unable to walk. Mrs. Fernandes, her family, and her neighbor, Mrs. Costa, nursed me back to health. A long time passed before I was strong enough to stand alone.

From my bed, I could see out the window. It was autumn. The leaves were turning and falling. A big fig tree was right outside the window. I studied it often. There were not many figs left, but I could see a fig on that tree where nobody else could see it. Mrs. Fernandes had several children. I would tell them, "Alfred," or "Tony," or whatever his name was, "there's a fig up that tree. Will you get that for me?" I wasn't supposed to eat it but they'd get it. I'd peel it and eat it in secret. It didn't do me any harm.

The children, sometimes on their way home from school, would pick a little bunch of seedless grapes, yellow as gold and sweet as sugar. They would sneak the fruit to me. I hid the grapes underneath the blankets. Every once in a while, when no one was around, I ate a few. I never noticed any bad result from eating those fruits. The only unusual reaction that I developed came from something else—a mistake made by Mrs. Fernandes. She, poor soul, couldn't read or write. The doctor had prescribed some liquid medicine for me to take by the tablespoon. Mrs. Fernandes put this bottle on top of the dresser. On the top of that same dresser was a bottle of rubbing alcohol—pure alcohol. That's what people used in those days. One day, as she couldn't read the labels, she went to give me the medicine and gave me a tablespoon of the rubbing alcohol instead. I took it, never thinking anything was wrong. The minute I got it down, I realized that something was different. I put my hands up on my temples. "Holy smoke," I yelled. "I'm on fire! I'm going to die!"

I hadn't stirred around so much for months. Right away she realized what she had done. She started crying. "Oh, my God, I've killed him!" she sobbed in Portuguese. "I gave him the alcohol instead of the medicine! Oh, my God!"

I guess she thought that I would die on the spot, but I didn't, of course, and she never made that mistake again. Maybe the shock helped me. Soon after that episode, I was strong enough to walk and finally to go to work again. I was in debt, and I was broke. I wanted to stay there in Hanford, to go to work to pay her back, but she would not have it. She wouldn't accept a dime, God bless her soul. There was nothing better for me to do. I came back to San Diego. It had been a little over a year since I had gone away.

When I returned I went to see my old boss at Western Metal, Paul Rayburn, Senior. He told me that he could give me a job but nowhere near the position that I had before. I would be starting back almost at the beginning again. I couldn't see that. I refused his offer, explaining, "I'm sorry, but a lobster is the only animal that walks backwards. I am not a lobster."

In a way it seemed a foolish thing to do. I was broke, and I was in debt, but I have always had a lot of faith. I walked out of his office. I didn't know what I was going to do, but I was sure that, with the help of God, I would find something.

I learned that my old boss, Joe Lawrence, had bought the fish business back from the fishermen. It was doing well and, in addition, he had taken on something new. He had made a deal with a man named Ed Merritt to clean and cut tuna and albacore for canning. Merritt started the canning of tuna here, as far as I know. He was interested in developing different aspects of the fish industry. The prepared fish was placed in a regular oven and was baked. It was canned by the use of a soldering iron. That's the way the industry here began.

Joe's bookkeeper wanted to go on a vacation; so Joe asked me if I would like to take his place for a month. "Joe, I can't do that. I can post and bill and ship, but I can't balance a set of books," I responded.

His reply was, "You just do that. When the bookkeeper comes back, he can balance the books."

I agreed under these conditions to take the job. Joe had been working hard and had not had a real vacation for some time. When the bookkeeper returned, Joe asked me to take his place, managing the business and working with the bookkeeper. He offered fifteen dollars a week to each of us, plus 25 percent of the net profits to split between us. We accepted; however, while Joe was away on his vacation the bookkeeper, Lee Foster, decided to accept a good offer in the grocery business up north. This left me in command.

The fish house gang, from American Fisheries. I don't know the exact date of this either, but it was after I went back to work for Joe Lawrence, following my attack of typhoid fever. I am in the middle, wearing the suit. The woman is the bookkeeper, whom I hired. At my left are a man named Alves and Joe Lawrence. The real name of the Lawrence family was Oliveira, the same as mine. When they came here, the brothers took the name Lawrence, because that was thir middle name. It was their father's first name.

I employed a woman, a good bookkeeper, for fifteen dollars a week. I kept the 25 percent of the net profit for myself.

When Joe returned from his vacation, he offered me an opportunity to go into business on a partnership basis, with himself, his brother, Frank, and Joe Miller.

I told him, "Look, I don't have any money. I've just finished paying my bills, and I bought some clothes that I needed. I'm flat. I haven't got a dime to spare."

"Don't worry about the money. I will get it for you." (I didn't know until recently that he had borrowed the money to loan to me.) It totalled $1,950.00. I had it made in fifty-dollar notes; so I could pay one note whenever I accumulated fifty dollars. It took me a long time to pay that money back, but it was paid.

Joe and Frank Lawrence left San Diego to open a branch wholesale fresh and salt fish market in Oakland. Joe Miller and I stayed in San Diego at the market at 841 Harbor Street, where the Eleventh Naval District building stands today. We occupied the site for over twenty-five years. We, also, bought a retail fish market at the corner of Sixth and E Streets. Mr. Miller operated the retail market, and I handled the wholesale market.

American Fisheries, September 1, 1930, 841 Harbor Drive.

Chapter VI

Mary

Although I was working hard during those early years, I had many good times. Our types of entertainment were inexpensive and simple. We were mostly on our own. The community was small. Once in a while someone gave a party. We played games such as "spin the bottle," "five feet in the well," "post office," and others. Sometimes we went to stock company shows or vaudeville. The Pickwick Theatre had been opened by then—1905, I believe, and the Savoy. The Savoy had Virginia Brissac as its leading lady for many years in the Savoy Stock Company. John Ray, her husband, also performed. The young people I knew in those days included the Palmer family, whose father, Scott Palmer, managed the Savoy Theater.

I didn't go with any particular girl. None of my friends did, either. We went in a group, boys and girls. Usually we decided on the spur of the moment. One of our favorite spots was the island of Coronado, across the bay. We'd say "Let's go to Coronado tomorrow or Sunday." We all would meet over there, after taking the ferry to Coronado and the electric street car to what was called Tent City.

Tent City was two rows of tents alongside the beach, with a roadway, and a sea wall. The tents were covered with palm leaves. People stayed there on vacations. Many came from Imperial Valley, to escape the heat. Others came from San Diego and around this area. Tourists also came from the East and Mid-West. Those tents rented for thirty to thirty-five dollars a week. There were concessions along the promenade. The young people walked back and forth, taking chances on the concessions. The rule was that if you won anything, you would give it to the girl that you were walking with. You see, after we got to Coronado, or wherever we were going, we paired off—but it was only temporary. I might go with one girl today and another next week. They all were nice girls. I never had a steady girl, though, except Mary—and that came much later.

The millionaire, John D. Spreckels, owned the hotel. He acquired it from Mr. Babcock and Mr. Storey, who was his partner. Mr. Spreckels came to Coronado in the late 1800s, when the town and the hotel were being developed by Mr. Babcock and Mr. Storey (who was from the Storey Piano people). He built Tent City in 1901 after he completed the hotel. It was "very fashionable," as Mary has said. There was a band concert nearly every night. Good singers performed. The musical entertainment was excellent. There was a ballroom, an open air swimming pool, and a children's pool, with a slide into the water. Those who sailed held regattas in Glorietta Bay, just below the hotel. There was a skating rink and ocean swimming. Coronado offered almost any type of entertainment that a person would want. Many wealthy people came to stay at the hotel. Mr. Spreckels paid for this entertainment for them. The rest of us got a free ride, so to speak.

On the Fourth of July there would be a barge placed in Glorietta Bay. At night from it would come a big display of fireworks. We'd sit on the Coronado side and watch. Mary and I stayed at Tent City one year on vacation after our first child, our son, Richard, was born, I remember.

Mr. Spreckels thought that by developing the Mission Beach Amusement Park and putting in things like "shoot the shoots," (a boat, on a slide, which zoomed down into the bay) and other amusements, the middle class would go over there, and the aristocrats would continue to go to Coronado, but it didn't turn out that way. He built that Mission Beach center in 1914, and it killed Coronado. Everyone went to the new place.

I didn't know ballroom dancing when I came here; so I took lessons from a man named Samuel F. Brockway. He had a big hall on Thirteenth and G, as I recall—it was the armory—and he held dances every Saturday night. The crowd that I went with, the fellows at least, attended those dances often. I paid him five dollars and got five lessons, or something similar. He or his wife would take us and dance us around the room, to practice before the dance started. After the rest of the people came in, they would introduce us to the girls; so we could dance with them. That's the way I learned.

I danced some at the Dreamland Ballroom, downtown on First and Ash. Another place where I went often was called Germania Hall, on Ninth and G. It was owned by the members of the German community of San Diego, but the place was available for banquets and parties. The building included a ballroom. A man named Morley Stanton held dances there twice a week, on Wednesdays and Saturdays. Sometimes the girls would come accompanied by their mothers. The boys always went alone. Occasionally a boy took a girl, if he had one, but in those days the girls and boys didn't run around together as much as they do today. Mr. Stanton would introduce us to the girls. We all had programs. We'd ask a girl to give us a certain dance. We'd put her name down. When that dance came up, you knew with whom you were going to dance.

Another thing—you were requested to carry a handkerchief in your right hand. When you put your arm around a girl, you didn't put your hand on top of her dress, because your hand might be perspiring. You took your handkerchief and used it against her back, in order that you didn't soil her dress. This is the way we were taught in our classes.

Sometimes when a dance was over, or even before it was over, a boy might ask a girl if he could take her home. If she were with her mother, she would ask her mother for permission.

I remember three sisters who came with their mother to these dances. I was stuck on the middle one for a while, but I was careful to dance with all of them. They weren't Portuguese. Portuguese girls didn't usually attend that type of dance. In business,

I associated more with the other people; so I went to many of their affairs. Sometimes this girl's folks would invite me to come for Sunday dinner. I went to church with them a few times, not a Catholic church, either; I think it was a Baptist. It was on Eleventh or Twelfth Street, below Broadway. The father's name was Brown, Stephen M. Brown, a well-known bricklayer. He was a Scot. Quite a few years later, after I was in business for myself, he did some work for me in the boilers down at the plant. One of his sons-in-law also became a bricklayer.

Mary never was a part of my early social life. In the first place she was twelve years younger than I was. I robbed the cradle when I married her. When we became engaged she was only fifteen years old. While I was running around with associates of my own age, she was walking with her cousins to the Saturday afternoon matinee or going to sit up on the balcony at Los Baños Pool to watch the swimmers. It cost a dime to go to the matinee at the Superba or the old Princess Theater. They showed cowboys and Indians, or Keystone Cops. Sometimes you were given a piece of china to take home. The pools, she remembers, were heated. The building was wooden. There was a springboard, and she and her cousins, and her brothers and sisters would sit all afternoon, watching the swimming and the diving. That was free entertainment.

At that time the Santa Fe Depot was across the street—a little frame building. The bay water came up almost to where the railroad tracks are today. Broadway was still a boardwalk that year that I was living with the Millers when their house burned down. The city used gas lamps and employed street lighters.

Another place that John Spreckels developed was the Ostrich Farm or Mission Cliff Gardens, at the end of the street car tracks on Park Boulevard at Adams. The grounds overlooked Mission Valley. There was a bandstand and ostriches which attendants rode. There was a bird house and pergolas and many trees and flowers. Admission was free. I think the San Diego Electric Railway owned the park. It closed down around 1930, after people started buying automobiles and going to other places. Mary went there, and so did I, but not together, in those early days before we were married.

My wife's mother was a pioneer in many Portuguese women's organizations. From an early age Mary shared in these activities with her mother and her aunts. Her father and her uncles, also, were active in Portuguese affairs. In 1914 my wife was queen of the *Festa do Espírito Santo*, the Feast of the Holy Spirit, a very important Portuguese religious celebration. I did not become involved in this affair until after we were married, but from then on, my wife and I were deeply involved for many years.

As I indicated earlier, I always suspected that Mary's attraction to me stemmed from the fact that I went into uniform and on military duty. She says that's not so. There's no disagreement, however, about the manner in which I acquired my uniform. In 1911, I joined the Naval Reserves. My commanding officer was a man named Don M. Stewart, whose name is familiar to many San Diegans. Mr. Stewart was born in San Diego on August 8, 1873, and passed away here on June 14, 1969. He was Postmaster here for many years. He wrote a book, *Frontier Port*, about his early life. Mr. Stewart started out with the California Naval Battalion, which later became the Naval Reserves. He joined the Battalion in February of 1894, I believe.

Another peculiar coincidence is that I also followed in his footsteps in one of my business activities. In 1900, he began working for a firm called McKenzie, Flint and Winsby. The firm name later was changed to Western Metal Supply Company. Mr. Stewart left Western Metal in 1906. I went there a few years later and stayed until I suffered my typhoid fever attack.

Our training exercises were held in the armory at the foot of Twenty-eighth Street. Each summer we went aboard the old gunboat *Marble Head* for a two-week cruise up and down the coast. For me, I was young and single, it was another place to go, another thing to do. The Reserves held some social affairs, also.

I had been in the Reserves for three years when World War I

broke out in Europe. This was after the Archduke Franz Ferdinand and his wife were assassinated in a place called Sarajevo. At the same time, there was a good deal of trouble in Mexico. Her president, Francisco Madera, had been assassinated the year previous. The United States would not recognize his successor. His name was Victoriano Herta. There was much hard feeling between the two countries. In Mexico there was a group opposed

Here I am, just another sailor boy, in 1914

to Herta. Everything was in a turmoil. Bandits roamed the border. Early in 1914, while plundering the town of Tecate, about forty miles from here, on the United States side of the border, they killed the postmaster.

The next thing I knew, my Naval Reserve group was ordered

to Palm City, on the border, fifteen miles from San Diego. Our job was to protect the fresh water supply of the area by guarding the reservoir there. A rumor was going around that Pancho Villa was heading north to start a revolution in Tijuana, and that one of their military projects was to be the seizing or poisoning of our water supply. Pancho Villa—his real name was Francisco— was a lieutenant of the man who was leading the fight against Herta. Villa had a terrible reputation. Our newspapers were filled with stories of his atrocities. Whether they were true or not, I can't say. All I know is that everybody in San Diego was pretty nervous. My wife recalls that everyone felt "as though it was wartime."

Before I went off to join my unit, I went to the Millers to say goodbye. After all, no one knew what was going to happen. I think I had dinner with them. There would be nothing unusual about it if I did have dinner with them, according to Mary. "He was almost a member of the family. He came often, to spend a Sunday with us, or a holiday."

She tells me now that, "When he would leave my mother would say, 'Oh, Lawrence will come here married, some day soon. You watch and see!'

"When she said this, it didn't set quite right with me, but I was only twelve or thirteen. What could I do? I thought to myself that if Lawrence ever did come to the house married, it would break my heart, but I couldn't tell anyone that. They would say that I was a silly child."

Her feelings were unknown to me until the time I went to her home in my uniform. Everything seemed different. Mary seemed different. She wasn't the little kid, running off to play with her cousins. She walked with me to the corner when I left. She wished me good luck and told me that she wanted me to come back soon and safe. She seemed concerned. I felt attracted to her, as though there was a bond between us which I, before, had never noticed.

I did something which, properly, I should not have done. I

found myself asking Mary if I could come to call on her when I came home. What I should have done, according to Portuguese tradition, was to go to ask permission from her father first. She said yes, and I went away, thinking of Mary. That, incidentally, was the last time we were alone together—if you can call it being alone when you are standing on a street corner—until we were married.

Our naval reserve unit at the border in 1914. I am in the white uniform, standing on the platform. The man at my left was named Scotty Hanes. He was an officer in the Coast Guard. Don Stewart, our commanding officer, was at my right, in the background, about four heads away. The sailor in the middle of the group below me was called Dutch. I never knew him by any other name.

At the border we picked up many Mexicans, but none of them were part of any plots against the United States. These people were scared and running away, for their lives. I was the only one in our group who could speak their language; so I was the interpreter.

Our company commander would give them a hearing. Usually the prisoners were interned in a compound at Fort Rosecrans, on Point Loma. Some of them tunneled under the fence to escape but usually were picked up. When the turmoil died down a few months later, we sent them back to Tijuana.

My military career was ended. I did not re-enlist. By that time, I was in business for myself and about to marry. I no longer had the time for the Naval Reserves. In a way I regretted this, for I enjoyed the life in the camp. Living in the tents, drilling, going on the training cruises appealed to me.

By the fall of that year, I was back in my wholesale fish market down at the waterfront. I, also, was dating Mary.

I had never thought seriously of getting married, although a good many people had me married a dozen times over, but that was their idea, not mine. I always had it in the back of my mind to get married someday and to have a family—to realize my dream of being able to offer my children all the opportunities that I had missed—but I never had any one girl in mind until after I started going with Mary; then I got down to business in a hurry.

At Christmas I surprised her with a present of a pair of long white kid gloves. She had never owned a pair of kid gloves. She was pleased. She thanked me over and over. When she finished, I told her that I had something else for her. I put a ring on her finger and asked her to marry me. That stunned her. She pulled it right off, saying, "Oh, Lawrence, you'll have to go ask my father first."

Her father accepted me, and her mother approved, and so did everyone else in the family; so that was it. The ring went back on her finger to stay. We were engaged. As I said, she was fifteen. I was twenty-seven years old. I was not making much money, but I was sure that I could support a family.

For some time I had owned the stone in the ring I gave Mary. I often ate at a certain restaurant on Broadway. I don't remember the name. The lady who operated the restaurant once showed me a diamond that she wanted to sell. I bought it. I wasn't engaged at that time—I wasn't even going with anyone steady. I bought it just to have it.

When I became engaged, I had the stone put in a ring. I think I had it done at Joseph Jessop's Jewelers, which then was between Broadway and E. He'd been in business several years and had moved at least once. He came here from England, if I recall correctly.

Our engagement lasted from December until the following October. There isn't much to tell about that period of time in our lives. Even though I had lived under the same roof with Mary years earlier, and even though we had known each other for many years, the customs had to be observed. The one time we had been alone together was enough, really too much. Whenever we went out, her brother went along or her sister, or her cousin. Sometimes it was her uncle.

On October 3, 1915, we were married in the old St. Joseph's Church, on Third and Beech Streets, where St. Joseph's Cathedral now stands. That was the same church where Mary was baptized and confirmed. She even remembers when Father Antonio Ubach, he was one of San Diego's most famous priests, served there. Actually he originated that church in the 1870's. The first brick building was completed in 1894.

Father Ubach was the same priest who was in Old Town for many years and helped the Indians whenever he could. When the woman who wrote the book, *Ramona,* Helen Hunt Jackson, described the priest in the book, she took her description from Father Ubach. My wife was only a small girl when he served at St. Joseph's but she says he stands out in her mind. "He wasn't a very tall man, but with a dark complexion. He had a beard and a mustache. They were gray—black and white mixed."

When he passed away, in March, 1907, he had one of the biggest funerals that this town has ever seen. The Indians came—everybody came—most of them couldn't even get into St. Joseph's. He was buried at Calvary Cemetery in Mission Hills. It was the Catholic cemetery then.

According to my wife we had a "small wedding." It seemed big to me. Her mother fixed a breakfast afterward. Later, we took a train to Los Angeles and stayed overnight. The next day we went to San Francisco. I was a delegate to a fraternal con-

Mary and I, on our wedding day. People often ask, "How is it that you are sitting down and she is standing?" I tell them, "I had a very hard day."

vention. The San Francisco Exposition was open at that time, also. There was a great deal to see and do.

Mary had never been out of San Diego. I had traveled a fair amount, but I'll tell you, even I was startled at one of the events which occurred on our honeymoon.

We had reservations at the Menlo Hotel in Oakland. When we checked in we were in a rush because we wanted to attend a big affair of the fraternal convention that night. Mary was in front of the mirror in our room, fixing her hair or something, I don't know what. I was bringing in the bags and starting to unpack when that hotel began to shake. It swayed over and back again, before settling down. We thought for sure it was going to go over and never right itself.

It was a frightening experience. We were up eight or nine floors. My wife had never been in that tall a building before. Neither of us had ever felt an earthquake of such magnitude. We held our breath for a moment, but then everything returned to normal. (We learned later, that although the earthquake was severe, there was no bad damage.) We hurried to get dressed for the big ball that night at the auditorium where the convention was being held. There the chief topic of conversation was the earthquake.

We visited San Francisco and the exposition. We called on my aunt and uncle and cousins who lived in the bay area. On the way home, we stopped to visit my sister, who had married and moved to San Luis Obispo to live. Her husband was a farmer. His name was Manuel S. Brum. They had ten children and raised eight. When he passed away, my sister returned to the San Diego area. Later she went to live in La Mesa. Most of her children and grandchildren live around San Diego, near her.

When Mary and I returned home we moved into a house on Columbia Street at Ivy, in the Middletown area. I went back to my wholesale fish market. Mary decided that she wanted to go to work, also. She thought that this would be of some help to us. I went along with this arrangement for five or six weeks, but I didn't like it. I told my wife, "This won't do. You stay home. Take care of the house. I'll take care of you. You're the boss from the front door in. From the front door out, I'm the boss."

She agreed. That's the way things have been run all through our marriage.

Chapter VII

The Ice Crusher

Over the years, our partnership discovered that maintaining the wholesale and retail fish business was a struggle, both in San Diego and Oakland.

Competition and credits were our worse enemies. We shipped fish all over the state of California and sometimes to New Mexico and Arizona. Our branch in Oakland, also, had quite a struggle, due to fierce competition from a firm called A. Paladini, which operated in San Francisco and Oakland.

We packed the fresh fish in wooden cases because the fish must be iced. There were no paper cartons at that time. To buy the lumber was too expensive; so we bought shoe boxes from the shoe stores in town — whatever size we wanted. These were wooden boxes, that boots came in, with a lid. We would put ice on the bottom, pack a layer of fish, and a little more ice, and so forth. We would fix and pack from fifty to one hundred and fifty pounds in a box. The final layer would be composed of ice. After putting the ice on the top, we nailed the cover. That's the way we made our crates at first. Later, when the business grew, there weren't enough shoe boxes to be had, so we bought new boxes.

Credits, or collections, were bad. We extended credit but didn't get the money back. If we asked for it, the people would claim that the fish didn't arrive in good condition. They refused to pay· the full amount. It was a continuous battle and little profit. I could see that this business would never produce the financial security for which I was striving; so I began to look for other methods of making a living.

Even though my business provided me with many headaches, it also gave me some advantages. I was right there on the waterfront. I could see the growth of the fishing industry, the changes that were taking place, and the new needs and new potentials which were emerging. Particularly as World War I ended, the picture began to change. The old relaxed days were vanishing. Mechanization was emerging. Some picturesque personalities disappeared.

When I first was on the waterfront there were characters such as the Italian named Zolessi, who had a little double-ended sailboat he'd used for years. His sons were fishermen, with power boats, but he wouldn't fish with them. He'd sing and sail and sing and row. Sometimes his sons would tow him out to the point. From there on he was by himself. He'd stay out a day or two and come back with a catch, singing at the top of his voice. The fish must have liked his singing for he always had good hauls, and he was never still. Often you couldn't see him, but you could hear him all over the harbor.

There was one Chinese left on the waterfront when I came. We called him "the Chinaman." Everyone called everyone else by his nationality in those days. Everyone was something. He had a little junk, the Chinaman did. He lived in it and fished from it. He kept it out in the bay. I don't think that he ever left the area around the bay. When he needed to come ashore, he'd use a small boat which he owned. The junk bobbed up and down out in the bay while he was gone. He fished every day, Saturday and Sunday and all, especially in the lobster season, when he was setting traps all the time. One day I realized that I hadn't seen him for a long time. Whatever happened to him, I don't know.

World War I helped the tuna industry. Tuna was purchased by the government for the armed forces. I remember that by about 1920 there were several canneries here. There was Van Camp, a corporation established by the Van Camp family. Their main office was in San Pedro. San Diego was a branch. Westgate was owned in part by Wiley Ambrose. He was the president of the firm.

The Steele Packing Company was owned by a man with the same name. He founded the cannery. I believe that he was the first man to pack fish in San Diego, but that was not tuna. He packed sardines. He had a cannery on Point Loma. Sun Harbor was founded by men named Cohen and Hopkins. Sun Harbor took over from them. Del Monte came here. It, also, was a corporation and its plant in San Diego was a branch of the corporation. People's Fish Company was another local firm. Joe Azevedo owned San Diego Packing Company. Star Kist was started out with the name French Sardine. Their main office, also, was in San Pedro.

Packing by hand started around 1911, or so. It was being done, as I told you, when I was working for Western Metal and when I first came back to San Diego, after being sick with typhoid fever.

The canneries didn't own any boats at that time, but later they began financing the operation and the construction of boats. They acquired interests in many vessels. This insured a cannery getting an adequate supply of fish.

The Italians were already here when I arrived, but the Japanese came later. One of the first Japanese whom I remember being in the fishing business was a man whose name was Kando. That's all we ever called him. When I was in the fresh fish business he started to import fish products from Mexico. He opened a fresh fish market. A man named Dikas, who was Greek, worked for him for many years managing his business.

Just before World War II, Kando disappeared, and we never heard a thing about him again. There was a rumor that he was deported for espionage, but nobody knew for sure. His business dwindled, even though Dikas tried to keep it up. I think Kando had a boat. I don't remember what happened to it.

The Japanese had a strong fleet here, although they didn't own more than half a dozen boats, all with Japanese crews. The Japanese seldom sailed on other vessels, and no one else ever sailed with them. They had fine boats, with excellent electronic equipment.

In my opinion, the Japanese were the best of all the fishermen, and their boats were unequalled. As I mentioned, there was talk that they were espionage agents in disguise. A rumor persisted that the Japanese had planned to invade us from the Gulf of Mexico. They were in the shrimp business there and were very strong in the tuna fishing there and on the Pacific Coast of Mexico. The rumor said that they had it all set up to take California, and that they planned to open up the Gulf by dynamiting all of the irrigation projects that held back the Colorado River and the waters of the Gulf. This would have flooded the Imperial Valley and ruined the railroads and highways.

It did turn out later that many of their fishing boat captains were high navy officials, but the bombing of Pearl Harbor was not the success that the Japanese expected. Something went wrong. They didn't try to take California. Many of their boats went to Mexico and stayed there for the duration of the war.

Long before all this happened, though, back in the days when the fishing industry was booming after World War I, I observed one interesting fact. Little improvement had been made in the methods of preserving fish. Fishermen, going out on longer trips, began buying ice in 300 pound blocks from the local ice house, Union Ice Company. They carried these blocks to the ships, loaded the ships and proceeded out to sea. From time to time, as ice was needed, the fishermen would break it up by hand with ice picks.

Eventually the fishermen began having the ice ground in the market and taking it in boxes down to the end of the wharf, where they let it into the boats with a hoist. With the elapse of time from the market to the boat much of the crushed ice melted. It didn't last as long as it should. It seemed to me that there must be a better way to handle the icing of the fish.

One day I developed a plan whereby I would rent a site on the dock where I could install an ice crusher big enough to take a 300 pound block of ice. If the crusher were mounted high enough so that the crushed ice would flow by gravity into the boats, it would save a great deal of time, thus keeping the ice from melting so rapidly.

I looked around, found a spot, secured a lease on it, and signed a contract with the Union Ice Company, which owned the property. Union Ice Company was situated at First and I Streets. I negotiated my deal with Al Burd, the manager.

After that action was completed, I needed $1,000.00 to buy the ice crusher and motor and to pay for the installation. I resembled the man who had all his house plans drawn and was ready to build, but discovered he'd forgotten to raise the money. I didn't have any money. I couldn't borrow it from the fish business. The business didn't have it. I had another responsibility by that time, also. Our first son, Richard Lawrence Oliver, had been born on August 1, 1916, at home in a house we were renting on Columbia at Beech Street. Mary had a doctor named Elliott. Richard was a strong and healthy baby. We were proud and grateful. With our next child we were not so fortunate.

My added responsibility made me anxious to improve myself business-wise. I was positive that the ice crushing firm would turn out to be a financial asset. I sought a way to raise the capital. I did not have to look far. I had some good friends, thank the Lord, who never failed to assist me when I needed them. One friend was Jim Bregante, an Italian man, who owned a wholesale fresh fish market. His niece, Katherine, or Katie, married a man named Mike Ghio, a fisherman. Many years later, after he passed away, she went into the restaurant business with her sons. They began the famous Anthony's Fish Grottos here.

I approached Jim to tell him my plan. "Come with me," he told me. He took me to his office and he said to his bookkeeper, "Give this Portuguese a check for $1,000.00." God bless that man. I will never forget him and all of his kindness to me.

I purchased the crusher, installed it, and started in the busi-

One of my ice crushers. This, and the following picture, were taken in the summer of 1931.

Crushed ice, from one of my machines, is shown here, being fed into a boat.

ness of furnishing crushed ice to the fishing boats. This was in the year 1918. I built a platform which was the height of the ice truck, in order that the truck would back into the platform and slide the ice off. We'd drag the ice by the end to the crusher, which would take a whole block at a time. We'd tumble the ice into the crusher. The crusher would grind the ice and shoot it down into the boat.

I charged a nickel a block for crushing. This was about a dollar a ton. I used this method until the boats got to be so big that I couldn't crush the ice anymore, because it wouldn't run by gravity. Especially at high tide the boats would be too high for the crusher to function.

In order to solve this problem, I leased space on the old Spreckels Dock, where John Spreckels had built the coal bunkers which formerly furnished fuel to the steamers when they came to port. As coal wasn't being used any more, I rented space in the coal bunkers wharf. There I installed two crushers. I had an elevator that went up twenty-five to thirty feet. We'd run a whole block of ice into the elevator, which would take this up to the crusher. It was at the top. The ice would tumble into the crusher and be ground, then it would fall by gravity into the boat. I kept the old crusher there, too, to ice the smaller boats.

There were many advantages to my method. It eliminated the storage of boxes of ice, saving space in the holds, and also eliminated the chore of breaking ice by hand at sea. It economized on ice, too, because the crushed ice hardened up and made a crust in the boat. The crust sealed. Thus the ice lasted for a long time. Some of the big boats took five or six hundred blocks of ice at a time.

This was my first real business all by myself. It was a success for many years, increasing at a rapid rate from the time I began. Soon I had enough money to repay Jim Bregante. I made out a check to him for $1,000.00 plus 7 percent interest, and I took it to him. He was standing in the doorway of his establishment when I went up to him, saying, "Jim, I don't know how to thank you for loaning me that $1,000.00. I am able to repay you now. Here is your check. If there is anything I ever can do for you, just name it."

There's where I got a shock. He took the check and studied it, peering over his glasses. I still can see him standing there, looking at that check, with a frown coming over his face; then he tore it up and threw it at me, saying, "You damn Portuguese! I loaned you $1,000.00, and that is all I want back."

I didn't have to be told twice. I thanked him, said I was sorry, went back to my office and made out another check. When I

This was one of the first swordfish that I remember being brought into San Diego. This was about 1910, I would say. Left to right, the men in the front row are: Manuel Silva, Barlou Estagnaro, Manuel Gomes, Angelo Ruiz, myself, John Monise, and Tony Scartich, the man who caught the swordfish.

returned to give it to him, he remarked, "That's all right. Any time I can help you, just ask me."

Another thing that bothered me was seeing the fishermen hoisting fish with a block and tackle by hand onto the wharf in front of our fish business. This occurred when they returned from sea with a catch to unload from their boats. I decided that it would be more feasible to put a power hoist on the wharf, where I could make a charge. I hired a disabled army man to run the hoists. It didn't require much physical effort. He could sit down and run them both. I put a house on the top. Both controls were there. He could see each of the hoists, which were situated on each side of the dock.

Whenever the fishermen had loaded a box full of fish they would signal to him. He would hoist it up out of the boat and let it down. He had complete control and could operate either hoist or both, using both hands at the same time if he wanted to do so. This was a time and labor-saving device. It, also, was a little easier on the fish, for there was not apt to be so much damage.

Occasionally, in the old days, the commercial fishermen brought in a swordfish. To the best of my recollection, however, commercial swordfishing did not start here until some time in the twenties.

Fishing for swordfish takes special equipment. Also, the swordfish usually are not caught close in to shore. San Diego's swordfishing techniques were borrowed from the east coast. The fishermen there, off Gloucester and Boston, Massachusetts, and similar places, had small boats. When they harpooned a a swordfish, they would tie a small keg on the end of the line and throw it overboard. The fish would fight the keg. Meanwhile, the fishermen would go away and fish in some other locality. Later that day they would return. The swordfish would be tired, sometimes dead, and they could bring it into their boat without danger to themselves.

Back east, the fishermen also placed a big plank on the bow of the boat. It protruded about sixteen feet past the boat. They fastened the end of the plank to the mast and attached a cable on each side of the plank. When they saw a swordfish, they got the harpoon out and walked to the end of the plank. From there they harpooned the fish; otherwise they would never catch him. Once that swordfish heard the motor or saw the boat, he would be off. He wouldn't stand there, waiting to be caught.

Eventually, a man named Seros Dutra, who fished for sword-fish in the east, came to San Diego. He used the same methods that he had employed on the east coast. He put the plank on the boat, harpooned the fish and tied a barrel to the end of the line.

Everyone watched what he did. The fishermen decided that he had a good technique. Soon, practically every small boat going out of the harbor had a plank on the bow. If you looked for them today, you would still see the planks on the boats. In later years, the sports fishing boats adopted the same procedure.

The boats that went out, though, still were tuna boats. This was the type of fish they were seeking. If the fishermen managed to catch a swordfish, that was well and good, but they never went out looking only for swordfish. That would not be economical. Swordfish are not a fish that run in schools, such as the tuna do. You don't see great numbers in one area at one time. You may see one or two, but that's all. I never knew anybody who was trying to make a living by fishing, who fished only for swordfish.

Years later, after I became a boat owner, one of our boats was rammed by a swordfish when she was out to sea. We didn't know it until we put the boat up for painting. We found the bill of the swordfish rammed about four inches into the plank—that was a double plank, too. The boat never leaked because the bill was stuck in the hole. The swordfish had left a long time earlier. I don't know what happened to him. I think the name of our boat having this encounter was the *Belle of Portugal*.

Chapter VIII

Branching Out In Business

I was doing well with the ice crushing and with the power hoists, but the partnership which Joe and Frank Lawrence and Joe Miller and I had formed, had never improved, either in San Diego or Oakland; so we decided to split up. Joe and Frank Lawrence took the market in Oakland and Joe Miller and I kept the one in San Diego, which we operated for a few more years without much success.

One day I proposed to Joe that we quit the business, but he was not much in favor of the idea. He encouraged me to continue. I did this for another year, but the trend was the same. One day, I told him that the only way for him to stay in business was to buy me out.

He asked me to put a price on the business. I did, so much for the wholesale and so much for the retail. He decided that he would take the retail; I should keep the wholesale and pay him the difference. This I did, also, and when the deal went through, I was broke.

I discontinued the fresh fish end of the wholesale business and went into the salt fish trade. When the fishermen would catch more fish than they could sell to the fresh fish markets, I would buy it, salt it, and eventually sell it. There was a very good market for salt fish among the Portuguese people living in California. Later, I shipped several carloads to Massachusetts, where there were large colonies of Portuguese people. This type of operation I found to be much more profitable than the wholesale fresh fish business had been.

As I worked along building up the salt fish enterprise, I began to see the need for some improvements in the salting process.

After studying the situation, I came up with some innovations.

Up to that time the fish had been salted and held in brine until it was to be sold. Then it would be drained and put in the sun to dry. If it happened that we had a drizzle or rain and no one covered the fish, the sea gulls would get on the moist fish and pick at it. They destroyed many fish in this manner. What they left looked terrible. Also, when the fish was dry, it was wrapped in second-hand burlap bags, which were not very clean. The fish had a certain amount of oil. The oil would pick up the dirt and dust from these bags. This made the fish look bad. It could be washed and cleaned up some, but it still looked bad. This was detrimental to sales.

This is a giant sea bass, or jewfish, as we called them many years ago. I don't remember the name of the man who caught and brought it to me. I can't identify the boy at my left, either.

I decided to ship the fish in cases instead of burlap bags; yet I still had the problem of drying it out in the sun and the hazard of the sea gulls and rain damage. It was an exasperating situation. Every night we'd pile the fish which were drying, and we'd cover them; so that the dew wouldn't get at them. The next morning we'd uncover the fish and separate them, in order that they would dry evenly. This was a tedious, time-consuming process.

I never have been known for patience. I always want to get things done in a hurry; so I devised a dryer. It was sixty feet long and about six feet wide and about four feet high. It had two shelves which were like racks. We put the fish on the racks. One end of the dryer was open. In the other end I placed a fan, which drew air from the outside and blew it through the dryer. In three or four hours I could dry all the fish that I needed.

Also, I no longer kept the fish in brine. I experimented with refrigeration. I drained the fish for a day or two and then put it in a refrigerator, covered with salt, making a stack eight to ten feet high, the heighth of the refrigerator.

I kept the refrigerator at 34°, so that the fish wouldn't freeze. The fish held in there for months and months in perfect shape. I packed the fish, which was gold and clean, in the cases. Sales went up. The business prospered. I did very well until I became involved in what turned out to be my principal business venture —the fish meal business. I still had the ice crushers. They were prospering; so I turned the salt fish firm over to Mary's uncle, Frank Lawrence, who had returned to San Diego from Oakland and had no business of his own. He helped to run the ice crushers sometimes, also. He kept this business going until the time of World War II, when fish prices became very inflated. There no longer was a profit in the sale of salt fish, so he gave it up.

As far as the ice crushing concern went, I maintained it for quite a few years, until the late 1930's. About that time, another ice company came to town. It was situated at Fourteenth and Imperial, I believe. This firm wanted to sell ice to the boats, but had no place to unload it because I had the waterfront pretty well tied up. The new outfit thought of building a truck, putting a crusher on it and driving the truck alongside the dock, where the ice was crushed into the boats.

I had no way of stopping this because it was a city dock. This was down on the waterfront around the bulkheads. The company was small. The owner couldn't make enough ice. Soon the Union Ice Company started selling ice to him. That annoyed me. I had a contract with the ice company and had been buying ice for years from them. During that time I had many opportunities to go into the ice business myself, with people who wanted me to make my own. I didn't want to do this because I figured that both the ice company and I had a good deal.

A man named Smith was the manager at that time. I went to Mr. Smith and I told him, "You are hurting my business, because the ice you sell to him, you sell to me. If he hasn't got it, they'd come to me for it. You still are selling the same amount of ice."

I was aware of the fact that refrigeration on the boats was coming in fast and that the ice business would soon begin falling off. The ice company manager said to me when I went to him, "If you don't like what's happening, why don't you sell your business?"

"Do you want to buy it?" I asked.

"We might."

"Hold on," I told him. "I'll think it over."

I went out and figured the amount of money that I had made during the year previous. I added two years to it, as though I had been in the business for two more years and made the same amount of money. I calculated that at the end of those two years there wasn't going to be much left of the ice business. I also added in the cost of the equipment that I had invested in the firm and my lease for the property. I gave the ice company a price and the company took it.

They told me, however, "We won't pay you cash."

I knew that this transaction would be an income tax deduction on their part, but that made no difference to me. I was out of the ice crushing business.

(I have leaped forward here some in time, from 1918 to 1938. In between those years I engaged in many other ventures, some successful, some not so successful.)

When I discontinued my fresh fish business, after splitting up the business with Joe Miller, I was left with some surplus material—refrigeration equipment, steam boilers and tanks for cooking lobsters. I soon found a use for it.

At that time a young man named Charles Landers was working for another man named Sandoval, who had a Mexican fishing concession. Mr. Landers wanted to go into business for himself. I knew him. We both were on the waterfront.

He came to me and made me an offer to go into the lobster business with him. He furnished the money and I did the work. After taking out the expenses, we split the profits. It was a good arrangement and worked out well until too many others got into the same business. When it was no longer profitable, we quit. We stayed in it, though, for a couple of years. We went to Mexico for the lobsters. In fact, one boat I built, in partnership with Mr. Landers and Paul Ames, who also was on the waterfront, and one other man, whose name escapes me, was built mainly to haul lobsters from Mexico during the season and to fish local fish during the off-season. It was called the *Chesapeake*.

After I gave up the lobster business, and I had then started into fish meal in a limited fashion, and had the ice crushing concession, Charles Landers and Jim Bregante and I decided to open a ship chandlery—a store which deals in supplies and groceries for ships. We had a building facing the waterfront, where a man named Galant had his barber shop. Later we moved to the coal bunker dock. We thought that we would do a pretty good business. We constructed a new building on the wharf at the foot of G Street. We were there four or five years. It was not a very profitable venture. I think this was because the fishermen didn't want to buy everything from one source.

I had the ice crushing and fish meal business already on the waterfront. They figured that was enough for one person.

We called the place Harbor Supply. My brother-in-law, Horace L. Miller, was manager of the store for a while. It was between 1920 and 1925 that I had this ship chandlery in operation.

In the twenties I pioneered in another field, but I guess I was a little ahead of my time. Someone I knew came to me and wanted me to furnish the cash to start a liquid coffee making firm. Two men whom I knew, Victor Ratliff, who had a dancing school, and Edwin Price, the manager of Solar Aircraft, and I put up the cash to start the project. We rented a building, bought a big coffee maker, and a distiller, and some other items. We would grind the coffee, then perk and distill it. We bottled it in different sizes. I don't recall we had a name for it.

We sold it to stores here and in Los Angeles. We had the firm for a year and a half, or so, but we didn't make any money on it; so we closed it. It was an experimental thing. We didn't have enough exposure—enough publicity—to make it go over.

I, also, at one time in the twenties was a theater owner. The Cabrillo Theater, by the Plaza, in downtown San Diego, was up for lease. It had been opened for many years. Along with Mr. Ratliff and another man named Ahrons, I took over the management of the theater.

We showed first run pictures. I remember we had the picture, *Cimmarron,* here for several weeks. It was a record for San Diego at that time. It was the first talking western epic. There were one or two made before, but the sound was not good. *Cimmarron* was a very successful movie, made in 1931. It dealt with the land rush into Oklahoma Territory, if I remember correctly.

Eventually we gave up the theater. There was too much competition for good pictures. Several other large theaters here, the Pantages, the Fox, the Spreckels, all had headquarters in Los Angeles, and they received preference in the selection of films.

Chapter IX

Big Business — Fish Meal

From the time that we were married, until 1924, Mary and I lived in the Middletown area of San Diego. Middletown was the district which lay between Old Town and the present downtown San Diego. Richard was born in the second house we rented—on the corner of Columbia and Beech Streets. From there, we moved to Albatross Street, where we rented a large house. My wife's brother, Joe, had married; so we two couples moved in together, to share expenses. From this house we moved to 1363 Columbia Street, between A and Ash. There we stayed until 1924, when we bought our first home, in a new development area on Thirty-second Street, south of University Avenue. Our address was 3586 Thirty-second Street. Only recently I sold that house.

Those first few years of marriage were hard for both my wife and me. Money was scarce. I was working day and night. All the family responsibilities fell on Mary. It was at this time, too, that we suffered a tragedy — the loss of our little daughter, Elaine, born in 1920. She never was a well child. She had difficulty taking nourishment. She weighed six pounds when she was born. She weighed twelve pounds when we lost her a year and twelve days later.

This was very hard on my wife. She was young. She was alone with Richard and with this sick child most of the time. I was not at home as much as I would have liked to have been. As she has remarked often, this experience left a deep impression on her. "To this day, no one ever seems to know what was wrong with Elaine. She never developed, never sat up, never used her tiny legs. She was like a little doll. I guess it was a blessing that the good Lord took her to be with Him, but it took me a while to learn to think that way.

"I had made so many big plans for my son and for my daughter. I thought I was something—a queen or something. I could decide their lives, what they were to do and be, but here was Elaine, and there was nothing I could do to stop what was happening to her. For the first time, I realized what the words meant when I prayed 'Thy will be done.' I thought 'Mary, you are just too big for your britches; you've been thinking only of yourself, and what you wanted.' After that experience, I decided that you must take life the way it comes, day by day. I never made another plan for my children's lives. Whatever they were to do, whatever they were to be, that was it. We have been blessed, for the rest of our children and our grandchildren have been healthy."

It was a disappointment to us, also, when we lost my father. The only one of the children whom he ever saw was Richard. When Richard was a baby, my father and my stepmother returned to the Azores to live. My father was not in good health and had not been able to achieve any success in business in the States. He had tried several things, small farming, raising chickens and so on, but nothing really caught on. At that time, I was in no position to help him. I had a business going, but that was all. We only made a living, and we had the children. We had many doctor bills.

My stepmother passed away. I sent the papers to him to bring him here to live with us. It was all that we could do for him. By the time that the papers got there it was too late. A month and a half after my stepmother died, my father accidentally fell in the bay and was drowned. In later years, when I could have helped him, how I wished that he still was alive, or that I had made more money faster.

Our daughter, Doris Mary, and our son, Norman Lawrence, were born after we moved to the house on Thirty-second Street. Doris was born in the old St. Joseph's Hospital, on October 10,

This picture was taken soon after our son, Norman, was born, on September 10, 1929. Richard is holding Norman, while Doris sits beside them. Richard was about thirteen and Doris about six years of age at this time.

1924. Norman was born on September 13, 1929, at Mercy Hospital, the old Mercy Hospital, which replaced St. Joseph's after it was torn down in the mid 1920's. Now that hospital has also been replaced.

During those first ten years or so, we didn't even have a laundry tray in the house. Mary washed with a washboard and a tub. She did all her own housework, all the cooking, made all the children's clothes, was never tired or upset when I came home, and still managed to assist in church and Portuguese women's groups.

Often I worked until early in the morning. There was no Sunday off for me, particularly after I started my own fish meal business. Mary never complained or pried into my business affairs. I had told her that I wanted to be boss from "the front door out" and she respected this wish. Sometimes, many times, I have asked her advice, and found it valuable on every occasion, but she never volunteered. From the "front door in" matters were handled in a excellent fashion. I always knew that when I left the house it was in good hands. This was a wonderful asset for me.

Where my business was concerned, I never was satisfied. Always I was looking for something else, something new, something better. I was willing to try anything honest. That's how I stumbled into my big business, the fish meal business.

One day, a black man whom I knew came to me and inquired, "Mr. Oliver, why don't you go into the fish meal manufacturing business? You've got all the raw materials at your disposal if you want to go into it—no one else is doing it."

"I don't know a thing about it," I replied.

He answered, "I do, and I will go to work for you and show you what to do."

I knew what he was talking about. It was the processing of raw fish into fish meal for fertilizer and for poultry food. It had potential; however, I was in no position financially to go into another business at that time. This was around the year 1920.

I thanked him for coming to see me and told him that I would think the matter over.

He planted an idea in my head. I began to try to figure out how I could go into the fish meal business. There had been one business of that type in the city, but it had gone broke. The owners had built a large building, but the bank had foreclosed on the mortgage and now owned the property, which sat idle.

I wanted that property, but it was too big a deal for me to handle at that moment. I began to search for alternative ways of going into the fish meal business. Some people weren't keen about that type of business because of the odor, I learned, but that didn't discourage me. I kept looking around. One day I found a place on the waterfront in National City. It belonged to an Arthur Blackman. He lived in Coronado, but he had an office in Chula Vista. There was a shed on the property, with a mill and a steam boiler which could be used in the manufacture of fish meal.

I approached him with the proposal that he become a partner with me and throw in the location, building, and machinery. I would furnish the rest of the equipment, which I bought on time. I told him that we needed two more partners, one to drive the truck, and one to show us how to make the fish meal. Their cash salary would be small, since they would have to pay their share of the partnership. He agreed.

For the truck driver, we hired a man named Joe Yocum. Hugh Hutchinson, the colored man, came in to show us how to make the fish meal.

We needed additional machinery. I contacted a friend in Los Angeles, George Kurtz, who worked for Standard Steel, a big firm there. He came to San Diego, arranged for me to buy some machinery and helped me to set it up. We finally were in business in a small crude way, without the proper equipment. We didn't have the money to buy what we needed. Still we managed to manufacture a certain amount of meal, but it was inferior and hard to sell. We couldn't extract the amount of oil that we should have, but we limped along for about six months; then we had a near-fatal accident.

Hugh Hutchison, one night at the plant, fell asleep during his tour as plant superintendent and engineer. (We all worked long hours at that time.) When he awoke, the boiler was dry. It was burned out. He tried to put water in it, but the injector didn't work—which was a good thing for him. If it had worked, it would have blown him to pieces, along with everything else around.

We were without a boiler. Until it was repaired we were forced to pay to have the raw material taken out to sea and dumped. Soon after this episode, Mr. Hutchison left our partnership. We then hired an engineer named Ernest Hollander, who was of Swedish descent. A little later on Joe Yocum quit, so we hired Joe Chavez, my wife's cousin. He drove the truck for quite a while. He was an employee, not a partner. By then there was just Mr. Blackman and myself. The business was called Oliver Meal and Oil Company.

We hadn't paid any dividends, since we had to pay for the machinery before we could split any money. We, also, ran into a little problem concerning the odor from the plant. In National City and Chula Vista, when the wind was blowing in the right direction, the people would get some odors, but it wasn't an unacceptable situation. The business was going along slowly, but making some progress. We were making our monthly payments and keeping our credit in good standing. Suddenly Mr. Blackman decided that he must go to Mexico on a visit. He had some business interests there. I didn't know where they were. I didn't know what he was plannnig to do before he left, either.

He was gone for quite some time—three months or more. One day I received a telephone call from the bank with which we had done business in Chula Vista. The bank asked "what I wanted to do about the note?" I was puzzled. "What note? I don't owe you any money."

The bank representative replied, "That's what you think. Your partner borrowed $500.00 in the company's name and that makes you liable."

You can believe that this was a shock to me! I offered to pay the interest, but the bank refused. "No, you are responsible for your partner."

That's a lesson which I learned the hard way. I didn't want my credit damaged; so I went to the bank and managed to pay off the note and the interest; but I was "sore," to put it frankly. I didn't feel that Mr. Blackman had done the right thing.

When he returned I asked, "What's the idea? You borrowed $500.00 in the company's name without telling me a thing about it. I don't like that."

"Well, we're partners. I needed the money. I didn't want to bother you; so I went to the bank and borrowed it."

"Yes, but the bank tells me that I'm responsible. If you haven't got it to pay, I must pay."

He finally paid the loan back. That, however, did not satisfy me. I decided that for my own peace of mind I should get out of business with him and be on my own.

The First National Bank still had the mortgage on the Southern Redemption Company, the fish meal company which had gone bankrupt. I wanted that business now more than ever. I went to the bank, to try to negotiate a deal whereby I could buy the plant for the lowest possible price. The bank told me that it would cost me $20,000—$18,000 to the bank and $2,000 to the city of San Diego for the lease of the site where the building was situated and for a past due water bill. The bank said it would be willing to sell it on time, depending on how much I could put down and pay monthly. I told the bank representative that I would see what I could do.

I had no money. Everything I owned was tied up in the Oliver Meal and Oil Company. I returned to my old friend, Jim Bregante, and explained to him what I wanted to do. I told him that if he thought I was doing the sensible thing I would ask him for a loan of $1,000, but I would insist on paying interest. He gave me the loan without a bit of hesitation. As he patted me on the shoulder, he said, "I wish you good luck and more power to you. I think you will do all right."

His confidence and his encouragement meant the world to me. The next day I went back to the bank. I took a deep breath before I went in. I was asking for so much, and I had so little to put down. I reminded myself, "Faint heart never won fair lady."

"Here is my proposition," I told the bank official, "and it is the very best that I can do. I will give you $1,000 down and 7 percent interest on the balance. I won't pay anything for a year —not even interest. At the end of the year, I will pay you another $1,000 plus interest. I will increase the payment each year by one thousand dollars, if I make it. If I don't, you can have your plant back with all the improvements. I'll just walk out."

The man laughed, "You're kidding—that's the best you can do?"

I said, "I'm not kidding. That's all I can do. I want that plant and I think I can make it go, but that's the best I can do. I will need to make a lot of improvements before I can show any profit."

"Wait a few minutes while I go to talk to the president, but I don't hold much hope for you."

I stood there at the counter for fifteen or twenty minutes, first on one foot and then on the other. He came out again and asked me, "Are you sure that's the best you can do?"

"That's the only thing I can do. I don't even own the $1,000 down payment. I had to borrow that. You might as well know that, too. Either take it or leave it."

"The plant is yours," he said, smiling at me. His name was Whitcomb, I remember, but I don't remember his first name.

I went to my partner, Mr. Blackman, and told him that I wanted to break up the partnership. He took his building and his machinery, and I took my machinery and we split the money that we had.

I signed a lease with the city for the property on June 22,

1922. I was on my own in the fish meal business. The building was situated at the foot of what is now Beardsley Street. I kept a business there for forty years. It made me a well-to-do man. By coincidence, when I sold it, the contract of sale was dated June 22, 1962, exactly forty years from the date I first signed a rental agreement with the city of San Diego.

Jim Bregante's prediction that I "will do all right," proved to be correct. He lived to see that. The steps to success were steep, though.

When I moved my machinery into the new plant, I felt as though I were alone in a big enterprise, which I was. If I made any money, it was all mine. If I lost everything, I had no one to blame but myself. I had no one to depend on but myself. During the next few years, I worked hard, sometimes eighteen hours a day and on the weekends, with many setbacks because of poor equipment. It was second-hand. Oftentimes I had it tied together with baling wire to keep it running. Those first two years were especially hard. There were times when my morale was low, but never for very long.

I remember one day when I had worked about seventeen hours straight. Everything went wrong. Everything I touched was wrong. I had several breaks in the equipment. No matter what I tried, the machinery kept failing. I was so tired and so disgusted that I sat down on a pile of fertilizer, and I cried. "If I had someone who would take this plant off my hands, the whole damned thing, I'd give it to him; I'd walk out empty-handed and never come back," I told myself.

Nobody came. I didn't give the plant to anybody. I went back to work and worked some more. Things began to get better. Some good opportunities came my way. I made a little money and bought new equipment. Always I kept my credit good. Later I found myself doing big business. I made big money.

Once I got a little ahead, I had my friend, George Kurtz, come down from Los Angeles to help me to design conveyors and other equipment which had to do with handling the material.

It was a big building, a three-story building. It had a freight elevator. At first we hauled the materials in cans up to the top and started the processing on the way down, by gravity. This was too much work. Later, we brought the equipment down to the lower level. Whatever we took up, went by conveyors. As the business grew, I kept buying equipment and making improvements. As long as the fish canning industry lasted in San Diego, I had equipment with which I could process twenty-five tons of fish an hour. I could produce from 1,000 to 2,000 tons of fish meal a month. I was at one time classed as one of the largest manufacturers of by-products of tuna on the Pacific Coast and the largest in the State of California.

Our firm was known as American Fisheries Company. The plant was at 1810 Bay Front.

Money and new equipment, though, were not our only problems in the beginning. In order to make a success of the fish meal business, I found it necessary to embark on a program of educating potential buyers. This, at first, was hard to do.

In the beginning, we had to sell most of the meal to citrus orchards for fertilizer. There was not much tuna meal purchased for poultry feed purposes. The poultrymen used sardine meal. We had a long process ahead of us, education of the poultry raisers and others, before they began to use tuna meal for feed.

We hired a broker who lived in Ontario, California. His name was Sidney Hertzberg. He arranged tours. We'd bring poultry farmers from San Bernardino, Riverside, Fontana, Pomona, and other cities around that area to San Diego and take them to the plant to show them how the fish meal was made.

At first we hired two touring cars—a Buick and a Studebaker. We'd invite ten prospects from Riverside, or thereabouts, and bring them to San Diego. They would be given a tour through the Van Camp Sea Food Company cannery, where they saw tuna ships unloading and the cleaning, cooking, and packing of the desirable portions of the tuna. They were able to examine the residual material left, the dark meat, the heads, the tails, fins and bones and skin, all clean and wholesome, although not fit for human consumption. This waste from the cannery was loaded into trucks belonging to the American Fisheries Company.

We followed the trucks to our plant, where we showed the people how Oliver Brand Fish Meal was made. We employed a vacuum drying system, using low heat and no direct flame. This helped to retain the nutritive factors. Our trademark was registered and was the only one in California. Our meal was incomparable food for fowl and for stock. Also, we processed, from the tuna discards, a fine tuna oil, high in Vitamin D, which we sold as a food supplement.

After the tour, the visitors were taken across the Mexican border to Agua Caliente, where they were entertained at a banquet, and then were driven home to Riverside. We made customers out of almost every one of these people.

At first they complained that the tuna had big eyes and there would be too many eyes in the meal. I told them and I showed them that one tuna which weighs twenty pounds has only two eyes. "How many eyes," I would ask them, "do you have in twenty pounds of sardines?"

By about 1930, we were carrying the visitors by the bus load from their homes to San Diego and return. Our business increased over 40 percent due to the promotional trips. Our ratio of tuna meal being sold to poultry raisers went from 25 percent to nearly 75 percent.

At first we used burlap or jute bags, buying them in lots of thousands. We had them marked with our trademark and emblem. Later, we switched to paper bags. We also had sacking equipment installed.

I went from three or four people at the start of my business to having fifty or more at its height. I hired a chemist. His name was Roger Truesdale. He did all our testing for the fish meal and for our other businesses from the Truesdale Laboratories, Inc. of Los Angeles.

Initially, the oil was separated from the water by oil separators. The surplus water was thrown away. Later, the Van Camp Sea Food Company, of Terminal Island, developed a process to make solubles out of the water which was pressed from the fish. These solubles also were in demand for the manufacture of feed for poultry.

I went to see Mr. Van Camp and talked him into letting us use the process on a royalty basis. This was an expensive process, but it paid off well until the canners started moving the canneries to San Pedro after World War II. There was only one cannery left in San Diego and it had a reduction plant of its own, so that ended the fish meal, fish oil and soluble business for us. By that time, however, we had a meat and bone reduction department which had grown into a successful business of its own. This was another activity which I more or less fell upon.

Chapter X

Suing Uncle Sam

I was always looking for something which would fit in with my business. At one time I was renting space to a man who was named Theodore Bach. He was picking up bones and fat from butcher shops around town. He and his son had a couple of trucks. In the evenings they would segregate the material which they had collected. They would load it in another truck and haul it to Los Angeles, where it was rendered. We were his transfer point and would take his calls for him. It was a good arrangement for both of us.

Hard luck fell on him. I went to him and told him, "If you have to get out of business, I'd like to buy your equipment."

He agreed. I kept his driver and started rendering in a small way, although I couldn't recover all the materials that I should retain.

We cooked, ground, pressed and dried the bones. This included both meat and fat. We rendered the fat. After being dried, the rest was ground into a fine powder. The powder, also, was used for poultry feed. I kept improving the equipment as the business grew until I had a very good system. I could handle all the meat and bones from the butchers and the slaughter houses around the city and county, except from Cudahy Packing Company, which had bought out the Hardy plant when Charlie Hardy passed away. Cudahy processed its own materials. The only time that we obtained anything from them was when their equipment broke down. At those times they would give us a call to come to pick up the material.

We sold the grease to Pacific Soap Company, which had a large plant here. It was on Market Street.

Our two departments went very well together, as I said, until the tuna canning industry moved out of San Diego in the 1950's. We then lost the materials for the fish meal business and were forced to discontinue it. We relied on the bone meal after that.

As the years went by, I saw myself prospering slowly, but steadily. Yet, I felt that I could not afford to pass up any opportunities. Everyone came to me with brainstorms, and many of them seemed worth trying. One of my plant superintendents one day suggested that I go into the manufacture of agar for medicinal purposes. He knew how to treat the sea weed or moss that grows on rocks under the water in some coastal areas. A gelatine is made from it. This gelatin is used for bacterial collections. I had almost everything needed in the way of equipment to do this work, so I went into the business. We remodeled part of the building and began importing the moss from Mexico, but it was too expensive. We wound up importing from Japan. Our buyers were pharmaceutical houses, such as Parke Davis, Squibb, and so forth. We did all right until the Japanese started doing the same thing and shipping the finished product to the United States. As I couldn't compete with them, I quit and looked for something else.

One of my business ventures led me into a successful and enjoyable hobby—that of raising cattle. It started when a man approached me with a proposition to treat municipal garbage for hog feeding.

His name was John Princel. He had a process which he had patented. He claimed that I had the necessary equipment. At that time hogs were being fed raw garbage. This gives the animals trichinosis. Mr. Princel wanted us to manufacture some feed and to run some experiments to prove that there was no trichinosis in the garbage when he processed the material. We needed some hogs, a place to keep them, and a truck in which we could pick up the garbage because the city wouldn't deliver it to us. I bought a truck and put a man on it, to pick up the garbage. The city gave us permission to do this.

We rented a few acres of land in a rural area called Santee, named after a man of that name. It is outside of El Cajon. There was a house on the property. We bought a carload of hogs, built some pens for the hogs, and went to work.

The garbage was processed in cookers. We added some chemicals, then we ground it, making a meal. A supplemental, with a little grain, was included. This made a very good feed. There was no trace of trichinosis, either.

We became ambitious and bought another load of hogs, then we ran into problems. The neighbors began to complain and brought suit against me. I paid a fine and was given three months in which to move the hog farm.

I told myself that if I were going to be in this business it was going to be far, far away from the rest of the people. I didn't want any more trouble. I found a place on Camp Kearney Mesa, named after the army camp which was here during World War I. This was three miles beyond where Camp Elliott, for the Marine Corps, was situated during World War II—and it was three miles from the highway—395 it is now.

I purchased a total of 360 acres of rough land, mostly undeveloped, buying from several owners. One section had the remains of an old olive orchard. The rest had nothing except snakes, jack rabbits and sage brush. You could look for miles in any direction. There was nothing to see. I thought that my troubles were ended, but out there I wound up facing a more grave situation than I had in Santee.

Our first problem was water. In the beginning, we carried it. We dug a well in a creek bed but didn't find much water; so I hired a well digger. We drilled close to 1,000 feet and got a well going. It produced about fifty gallons a minute. We had no electricity out there. I used a Ford motor for pumping power. This produced enough water for the stock.

Later, I built a reservoir on the other end of the property. When it rained a good deal of water came down through the ranch, for it contained a large gully. I hired George Daley, who was an up-and-coming excavating contractor, from the Daley family, an old family here, to build an earth dam. The first year it filled up and went over. It never filled up after that year.

We moved two houses in for the employees. This was shortly before World War II. I had made many improvements by then. Ed Fletcher, the land developer, later our State Senator, came to me to take an option on the place, but it never materialized. Fletcher and I worked together later on something else, though, and that's a story in itself.

We were doing quite well. At one time, I had over 1,000 hogs. Our pork was of a fine quality and made wonderful hams and bacon. I sold them mostly to Cudahy, here, but I, also, shipped to Los Angeles. The hogs made quite a profit until the other hog raisers forced us out of business. Between them they contracted with the city to take all the garbage of San Diego for between three and five years. If I wanted to stay in business, I would have to take all the garbage of San Diego for this period. I could not do this unless the city would finance my putting in a large processing plant. The city wouldn't do that, so the garbage processing business was finished. I sold all my hogs.

Meanwhile, I had put a few head of cattle on the ranch. A nephew of mine, who had a dairy in San Luis Obispo, lost his lease up there, and he had no place to go. I offered him space on my ranch here, and I built him a milk house and a refrigerator for the milk, plus a hay barn. I, also, had a few head of Devon cattle—English cattle—and some horses. We put in a nice kitchen and a platform where we could put picnic tables and chairs. We could dance there. We often went horseback riding and had picnics on Sundays and holidays. Our family and our friends came out to visit. By that time, just before World War II, I was in a position to relax a little. My businesses were prospering and I could afford to spend some time away from them. Then came the war.

The next thing I knew, the government came to me and said, "We want your place. You move your cattle and all out in thirty days. We will give you $14,000 for it."

"Oh, no," I replied, "I've got almost $50,000 invested out there. I can't let you have that place for that amount."

"You can't do anything about it," answered the government. "If you don't like what we offer you, take 25 percent and sue us for the rest."

I said to myself, "Holy Moses, a little peanut like me should sue Uncle Sam? What shall I do?"

I saw an attorney named Jim Pfanstiel. He told me, "Don't worry. It's being done every day."

On his advice, I started looking for another place. This time I went forty miles east before I found what I wanted. I bought 2,200 and some odd acres of an estate which was for sale near the town of Descanso. I moved my cattle out there.

Meanwhile, my attorney went to work. We sued "Uncle Sam." We took an appraiser out to the Camp Kearney property and he appraised every foot of fence and every foot of lumber that was in the place—all the improvements. He came up with the figure of $55,000. That's what we sued for.

It took two years before the case came to the Federal Court here. The judge was from Seattle. We asked for a jury trial. The jury returned a verdict of $49,000. The government, also, was to give me 6 percent interest from the day it took the ranch until the day that it paid me.

The government then filed a brief for a new trial. It claimed that I had given Ed Fletcher an option for $40,000, and that was correct, but that was before I had put in all of the improvements. The judge wouldn't allow the brief. He said that the attorneys should have introduced the evidence earlier. The government threatened to appeal the case, but it never went to trial. A year later the government decided to pay me. The interest that it gave on the $49,000, more than paid my attorney's fees.

I still had the ranch in Descanso, which I kept for many years. I want to go into that part of my life a little more thoroughly later on.

Chapter XI

Fishing With A Silver Hook

Although I was associated with the fishing industry for the greater part of my business life, I, personally, never fished commercially. "I fished with a silver hook," as the saying goes.

Around the year 1925, I bought an old fishing boat. A man, whose last name was Mello, operated it for me for three or four years. He became ill and couldn't work; so I sold the boat. She was called the *Princess.*

About 1930, I built my first fishing boat. At that time two or three men would get together and build a boat. This was what I did. I went in partners with a fisherman named Manuel Silva. We built the *Amor da Patria,* or *Love of Country.*

Mr. Silva operated the boat, but at that time he was not an American citizen. You had to be a citizen in order to be a captain. We put another man in as captain, although Mr. Silva did all the work. The only time that I ever had trouble with a foreign country was over the *Amor da Patria.*

Mr. Silva and the crew were fishing one time off the coast of Mexico. The water was rough; so they came in close to shore to anchor for the night, thinking that they would be up and out of Mexican waters before anybody saw them. They did not have a Mexican permit. We didn't intend fishing inside the three-mile limit.

They overslept that next morning, and the Mexican revenue cutter came by and picked them up. We had almost a full load of fish on the boat. The Mexican government seized all the fish and held the boat for three months before we were able to get it free. It cost us, I think, a fine of $3,500. We worked through the

99

American Consulate in Ensenada. The representative did the best he could for us; still it took three months.

This happened not far from here, around the little bay of Santo Tomas, or close in there, near Ensenada, which was where they took the boat. Ensenada is about forty-five miles from San Diego. In those days, we didn't have to go far to fish. Most of the time the fishermen would start fishing from here and follow the fish down the coast. We never went further than Panama with our boats.

After I had that first boat built, I built the *Chesapeake,* with Charles Landers and Paul Ames as partners. I mentioned that before. I built both of those boats at San Diego Marine Construction Company. Our next, the *Shasta,* was about sixty-five feet in length, but she was built for tuna fishing. It cost about $75,000 to $90,000 to build each of those boats. They all had wooden hulls. I never owned a steel-hulled boat.

I bought an interest in a boat called the *Luisitania,* from Manual G. Rosa. He was a true fisherman and a good friend. He was a native of Pico, also. Mr. Rosa came here in 1923, with his fishing boat, the *Peerless.* There was nothing he didn't know about fishing. He pioneered many new techniques. He passed away early in 1972, and San Diego lost a fine citizen.

Mr. Rosa and I operated the *Luisitania* for a long time. Later, we remodeled and enlarged it. We stripped it down to the keel and built it up from there. We kept it for many more years. The work was done at a shipyard at the foot of Twenty-eighth Street. I don't remember the name of the yard. It is out of business now.

We made a good profit on our boats. We did well, especially with the *Luisitania.* In 1937, Mr. Rosa and I and his brothers built the *Belle of Portugal* through Campbell Machine Company here. This boat was 142 feet long and carried 350 tons.

After we got her started working, we built a sister ship, the *Picaroto,* the *Man from Pico.* These two were real tuna clippers, partly brine refrigerated and partly ice refrigerated.

Our last boat was the *Azoreana.* She was 100 percent refrig-

This was launching day for the Belle of Portugal, in 1937. She was the ship which burned and sank, in January 1967. One problem we faced as our boats grew older, was getting good crews. It isn't so much a question of money as it is the conditions aboard the boat. The newer the boat, the more accommodations for the crew. The crew also has much less work. This is a factor with which all boat owners must deal.

erated and the first boat that was 100 percent refrigerated to be built in San Diego. Mr. Rosa and I each put in 35 percent, and his family owned a small percent. For a time, Van Camp Sea Food Company had a small interest in the boat. The *Azoreana* was 149 feet long. If a boat was over 150 feet, the rule was that you had to have a licensed captain to operate.

All these boats were for hook and line fishing, which is catching each fish individually with a pole and a hook and line. We never built a purse seiner. A purse seiner is a boat built with a big net attached to a turntable. The net encircles and traps fish. Hook and line fishing was wonderful, although you had to go in close to shore to get bait, for the bait had to be alive. We used anchovies, small sardines and other available small fish. We carried bait tanks on board. We would make a setting for anchovies or sardines and take them from the net with a scoop, from which we would drop them into the bait tanks. The water in the bait tanks circulated all the time by the use of pumps which brought it in from the sea. After the bait would be in the tank for a day, the fish would start swimming around all one way, as if they were trained to do it. We took a tuna or some other fish, maybe a bonita, and ground it very fine, to feed to them. They would thrive for weeks on board.

The only electronic device we had at that time was what was called a "sound machine." This machine tells how far you are from the bottom, which is absolutely necessary. The insurance companies demanded that we have a "sound machine" on board.

During World War II, most of the fishing boats were requisitioned by the government. As fast as the bigger boats returned from sea after the war began, the government leased them. They wanted the boats which were between 100 and 150 feet. Our three largest boats, the *Belle of Portugal,* the *Picaroto* and the *Azoreana,* were requisitioned. The government leased the boats with an option to buy. Later it bought them outright.

Our boats were ideal for navy purposes in the Pacific. They

were called the "Yippee Fleet," because they carried the letters Y P for identification.

At first, the boats were used for patrol craft, to protect the Pacific coast and to watch for Japanese submarines. The bait tanks were stacked with depth charges and peashooters were bolted to the decks.

Later on, the clippers were employed to supply fresh water and food, fuel and ammunition to the hundreds of small islands which we had seized in the South Pacific.

The refrigerators, formerly used for fish, carried meat and other perishable foods. The tanks stored fresh water.

Another need was for men to run the boats. In February 1942, the naval headquarters in San Diego put out a call for help from the fishing community. A mass meeting was held in the Naval Reserve Armory. In one day, 600 commercial fishermen volunteered to serve in the Pacific aboard their former boats. Many of them found themselves in actual combat, delivering platoons of raiders to Japanese-held islands or ammunition to assault groups. I believe that a total of fourteen tuna boats from this area were lost during the war.

After the war, the owners were given the opportunity to buy back their boats. Most of them later regretted having done so; for the boats were in bad shape. Some of them never could be properly repaired.

World War II produced some important side effects in San Diego. It put an end to the Japanese fishing fleet. The canneries began to close down. Purse seining developed.

Many of the Japanese boats disappeared before the war began. As I have said, we saw several of them in Mexico. When the Japanese were evacuated to the internment camps for the duration of the war, their boats here were confiscated. I don't know if there are any Japanese citizens operating fishing boats in California now. I don't think that any fish from here. While they were here though, I bought from them. Everybody did.

As far as the canneries are concerned, the open-market policy we established toward Japan's fishing industry after World War II led to the fishing industry people being forced to devise new methods of saving money. One of the effects was that the canneries closed their branches here. The owners felt that all the fish might as well be brought to San Pedro; so they packed up and moved. Most of the fish caught by San Diego fishermen goes to San Pedro now. Van Camp formerly packed 300 tons of fish a day here. Van Camp left. Westgate bought the Sun Harbor and the Van Camp spaces and merged the two. Star Kist left for San Pedro. Two other canneries left, also.

Fishing was bad after the war was over. Bait became so scarce that most of the boats went to purse seining. Somebody came up with the idea. For a long time I was against it. I still am, frankly. I don't like the idea that everything you get in your net gets killed. To me, that's a terrible waste. Our boats, though, were obsolete. We had several meetings to discuss the problem. I finally agreed to the change.

We borrowed money to do the remodeling. It cost us $150,000 a boat to equip for purse seining. We equipped four of ours. We had to remodel the stern, build a turn-table and buy a big net. All these things are expensive. At first, all the nets came from Japan. The DuPont Company later started manufacturing nets. I think they still do.

Its easy to seine tuna because the tuna is a school fish. They travel in large hordes. When you discover a school of fish you encircle it with the net, close up the bottom and bring the net close in to the boat. Purse seining is an art, a trade in itself. We never did too well with it. Our fishermen were not accustomed to this method and soon our boats were too small.

Insurance on the boats became very expensive. We sold the *Luisitania*. When the insurance came due on the *Picaroto* we decided to cut the value down from $225,000 to $75,000 in value; so that the premium would be less expensive. After all, we figured, the chances were that nothing would happen. On her next trip the *Picaroto* hit a reef and sank. We lost another boat later. *The Belle of Portugal* was fishing ninety miles out of Panama during the last part of January, 1967, when she caught fire and sank.

Luckily, the crew was saved. We had a load of fish on board. The fish was insured. The insurance company, however, refused to pay for the fish or for the smaller power boat, called a "skiff."

The company said that the crew had reported only forty-eight tons of fish on board. Insurance rules call for "notifying shore," or calling ashore everytime you pick up one-quarter of a load on board. In turn, the shore notifies the insurance company. Thus the fish is insured.

Our crew did report the first quarter of the load before the telephone went out of commission. There were no other boats nearby which could relay the message on the additional tonnage. However, the captain had been able to save his log book and his license, which the court later accepted as evidence of the tonnage of fish caught. Our total loss was $324,000. The insurance company offered a claim settlement of $185,000, which we refused. We went to court. The judge ruled in our favor. The insurance company appealed the verdict, but the Appellate Court ruled in our favor. We and the crew waited three years for our money.

We fished most of the time for Van Camp Sea Food Company. As long as the company had a cannery in San Diego, we delivered to San Diego. After they moved to San Pedro, we delivered there. If any of our cargoes spoiled, I would use the materials in our fish meal plant.

My experience with the fish business has been extensive. I made some money and lost some money. I know I made mistakes. There are things I would do over, but since 1971, I am out of the fish business and I would never go back. I had many heartaches and headaches over it. Fishing is a lot of grief. Now, of course, it also has become "big business," with huge ships, which require great investments. There also is a trend to move both the ships and the canneries to Puerto Rico and Panama, both to save on operating costs and taxes and to be nearer to today's fishing areas.

Chapter XII

The Case Of The Missing House

When I talk about our early married life, I suppose that it could sound as though those days were pretty dull, but that's not true. We worked hard, but we had many satisfactions, Mary and I, during those years. Our children were growing. We made friends in the community—developed interests which gave us much pleasure—we had it hard, but we had good times, too.

I had always promised myself that my children would receive all the education and training that they needed and wanted. It seemed no time at all before I had a boy turning into a man.

Richard, our oldest, graduated from San Diego High School. He wasn't interested in going to college. From the time that he was a small boy, Richard wanted to work with his hands. When he was only ten years old he worked the hoist which unloaded the fish on the docks. He earned ten dollars a week. He did this on the weekends and vacation times.

His mother and I told him that, since he was working, he must pay room and board. He paid five dollars a week for room and board, and the other five dollars went into the bank. Actually, it all went into the bank. His mother saw to that, but he thought for many years that he paid room and board.

In 1937, Richard started working for me in the fish meal business. This was after he graduated from high school. I made him a foreman, although he was quite young, but I wanted him to have the responsibility. I told the other men what I was doing. I instructed them that if he didn't handle things right they were to tell me. He worked out fine. To tell you the truth, I was surprised.

One day, though, he came to me and said, "Dad, I want to go fishing."

We had just built the *Azoreana,* and he wanted to go out on her, but that didn't work out. He started on another boat, the *Navigator,* under a captain named Joe Rogers. Eventually he switched to the *Azoreana,* under my partner, Manuel G. Rosa. He fished for two and one-half years and saved a little money. I told him when he left that I would never ask him to come back to work for me. When he wanted to return, he could tell me. He decided to come back. I was hoping that he would. Richard managed the business for me for twenty years or more, until we sold it.

My son, Richard, with me, at the plant.

After that, he didn't want to work for the firm any longer; so he quit. He shopped around for something to do and settled down on a ranch near Cave Junction, Oregon. There he raises milk cattle. Richard has three children, Lawrence Richard, who's nickname is "Rick," Marie Leilane, and Thomas Patrick.

Doris, our daughter, graduated from Our Lady of Peace Academy, here in San Diego and from Mount St. Mary's in Los

Angeles. (Our Lady of Peace was established by the Sisters of St. Joseph in 1884.) Doris worked in San Diego for several years for an insurance company before she married a navy lieutenant named José Porto. They traveled a good deal. Doris has three sons, Joseph Oliver Porto, Andrew Oliver Porto, and Christopher Oliver Porto. Andrew is called "Drew." Doris is the manager of El Rancho Verde Country Club, owned by the Oliver family in Rialto, California. (Rialto is a small town in San Bernardino County. The people up there and the Chamber of Commerce say that the town was founded in 1887 and that the name is derived from *Rivus Altus,* the name of the Grand Canal in Venice.) I became acquainted with the town when our family assumed an interest in building the golf course there. This was in the 1950's.

Norman graduated from Point Loma High School. He attended St. Mary's University, in Moraga, California, outside of Oakland, for three years. He worked for me during the summer months also, while he was in school. After he discontinued going to college, he came to work for me in the fish meal plant, but he wasn't happy there. He doesn't like a place where he is confined. He and Richard are very different in disposition. One day he came to me and said, "Dad, I know you are not happy with my work here. I'm not happy, either."

"Well," I said to him, "what do you want to do for a living?"

"I don't know, Dad."

I told him, "You'd better go and find out," so he went. He shopped around a bit, also. He managed our golf course in Rialto for eight years and now has managed another in Costa Mesa for several years. He likes this type of work.

Norman has three children, also. They are Mark Lawrence, Renée Dolores and Stephen Lawrence.

My wife, who is the authority on the Portuguese customs in our family, would tell you that for Norman to give his sons my name for their middle name is traditional in the Portuguese homes, just as it is for a girl to give her sons her maiden name,

109

which is what our daughter, Doris, did with her boys.

Our grandchildren have always called us *Avó* and *Avóu,* which is Portuguese for grandmother and grandfather. Really they call us *Vavó,* and *Vavóu,* which is another nickname. Its like saying "grandma," or "granny" or something similar to that. They grew up doing it and never thought anything about it until one day two or three years ago when one of them looked at Mary and asked, "We call you *Vavó,* but you really are our grandmother, aren't you?"

One of the rules that my wife and I laid down early in our marriage was that one parent would never interfere with the other's actions toward any of the children. In private we could disagree but never before the children. We, also, were very strict, but our children got a good deal of affection and attention—not just from us, but from my wife's big family. Mary never had a baby sitter. Once in a while, if something came up, her mother took the children, but generally wherever we went, they went. We always spent our Sundays together after I began having some free time. Before we bought the ranch we would go on picnics, for rides, and visiting our family and friends.

No, those days in the early twenties and thirties weren't dull days, not by a long shot. As a matter of fact, we had some rather unusual adventures during that time. We took a Sunday ride one day in the early thirties. It resulted in what we call the "Case of the Missing House." Very few families have a missing house in their history, but we do.

Around 1920, we met an old gentleman who owned a house. He was elderly and had no means of support. We became friendly. I took to him. This was before this country had social security and other legislation of that nature. His funds were exhausted, and he was too old to work. Every once in a while I gave him a few dollars. He lived in National City, on Eighth Street. He owned a five-room house and the lot on which it stood. He had fruit trees in his yard. Occasionally he brought us apricots and figs and other fruits. He lived alone and didn't pay any rent; so it didn't take much of an income for him to get along. His name was Anton Perry.

He became ill. I took him to the doctor. He went often. He'd consult with me and make his appointments for when I could take him. I owned a car by then. This went on for ten or twelve years. He grew worse; at last he entered the hospital for treatment. I visited him. One day he said to me, "Lawrence, you kept me going for quite a few years. I have nothing to repay you with except my house. I am going to will this house to you."

After he was discharged from the hospital, he went to an attorney, and he willed the house to me. A year or two later he passed away.

It was a cheaply built place, with up-and-down boards. This was a type of house which was constructed often in those days—boards outside and inside, no plaster inside. There was good lumber, though, good redwood, that you couldn't get today. I tried to rent the place, but the city stopped me because it was not connected with the sewers. I closed it up and I let it stay unoccupied.

One day I went there and walked through the house. When I got to the kitchen, I saw that someone had dug a hole in the middle of the kitchen floor, about eight by six feet. Whoever it was had pulled up the wooden floor on top of the dirt and dug in the dirt for buried treasure. You see, this man had lived there for many years, and he didn't work. Someone figured that he had money buried.

Oh, that hole was deep, about four or five feet deep. I closed up the house. I didn't do anything about it. I forgot about it.

Later, on a Sunday, my wife and I and our children took a ride. We drove down to the Tijuana border and Chula Vista. "Let's go through National City," I suggested. "I want to show you the house that was left to us." I drove to the spot where the house was situated. When I got there, there was no house.

A goat was tied in the middle of the lot. The house had been taken quite some time earlier. Grass had grown up. The goat was grazing on the grass.

I went around the neighborhood, inquiring if anyone had seen anybody tear down the house—or if it had been moved away whole. Nobody knew anything about it.

I didn't do anything. The house was gone. It probably would cost me plenty if I tried to find out who took it. I would have more trouble than I would get out of it. I forgot about the house, but I kept paying taxes on the lot. A few years later I had a chance to sell it for $2,200. It was near the railroad tracks on Eighth Street.

Chapter XIII

The Days Of Wine And Song And Car Thieves

As I said, from our earliest married days Mary and I always had a good many outside interests. Among these were our church and Portuguese activities. We participated in many community affairs. Another interest which we shared in common was singing. Music and dances and songs are very important to the Portuguese. People in the islands sing a good deal. Every child learns the verses to all the old, old songs. Every so often over there, they have a party. They play the guitar and the viola, which is the native instrument of the islands. It looks like a guitar, but it's larger. I have the one which belonged to my father. I play it a little.

In September, in the islands the people pick the grapes and make their wine. The wine barrels are taken down to the seashore to clean them. The people put little pebbles and salt water in the casks and shake them, to remove the residue. After the barrels are cleaned, the fresh wine is poured into them. After all this is done, they have their party—eating and singing and dancing. They bring out the salt fish and cook potatoes. That's a party over there.

The people in the islands, also, have a festival before Lent. The men dress up as women. This is called the *Mardi Gras*. No women participate. The men go out in the streets and parade and dance.

Years ago, after I came here, I decided that I wanted to learn to play the violin. I struggled around with that ambition for quite a while, without much success. Later, I decided to take piano lessons. That meant that I had to buy a piano. I learned nothing there, either. Instruments were never meant for me.

113

One thing I always had, though, was a good singing voice. I obtained a lot of practice peddling fish here and singing to keep myself from being scared to death when I was a child in the old country. In San Diego, long before I was married, I sang as a hobby. I was once a minstrel in a show at the Spreckels Theater soon after it opened in 1912.

I, also, was a soldier with a sword during a production of *Julius Caesar* at the old Fisher Opera House, which became the Isis Theater after Madame Katherine Tingley bought it in 1902. That was the start and the end of my dramatic career.

Mary decided to take voice lessons when our youngest son, Norman, was a baby. I was studying at that time under an instructor here in town named Edwin Thill. I went from work to my lessons before going home. This was while we still lived on Thirty-second Street.

Mary said to me one day, "I'd like to take lessons, too."

"Fine," I told her.

She recalls carting the baby along when she went for lessons. "Norman would sit on a rug at the Thills. We gave him toys to play with, to keep him amused, while I took my lessons. The Thills were very understanding people. They realized that I had to take him with me. I had no car. My family lived downtown, clear past the Thills, who were on Lincoln Avenue in Hillcrest. We've often said that maybe that's the reason that Norman turned out to be musical. He's the only one of the children who did."

We sang together in church choirs at Saint Joseph's Cathedral; at Saint John's, at 1638 Polk Street; at Saint Patrick's, on Thirtieth Street in North Park; at Our Lady of the Rosary, 1659 Columbia; at many different churches and for organizations and for special events.

Mary was always with me, except when I sang with the Elks. I had joined the Elk's Lodge Number 168 in May 1925. They had a singing organization called the Elk's Chanters. It was directed by a Mr. Dibble. One evening, he asked anyone who could sing to join the Chanters. I tried out and became a Chanter; however, I felt that I should have some vocal lessons. That's when I started to go to Mr. Thill. After Mr. Dibble died, Mr. Thill became the Chanter's director. He, also, was director for many years of the choir at the Cathedral. He was a wonderful director and an outstanding man. His wife, Katherine, was an excellent accompanist and a fine lady.

The first solo I ever sang in my life I thought was going to be the last. The Chanters were presenting a Mother's Day program in the Elk's Lodge Room. I was chosen to sing a solo—one of those Irish mother's ballads. I don't remember the title. We gathered in the choir loft on the night of the program. The time came for my solo. Mr. Thill nodded to me. I walked to the front of the loft, right behind the railing, which came to my knees. Mrs. Thill played the introduction. I opened my mouth. Nothing came out. She played that introduction three times. Finally some voice emerged. I got through in fine shape, they told me afterward. All through the number, though, my knees were knocking against the railing. I was sure that they could hear the rattling down below.

Mary belonged to the San Diego Morning Choral Group and the San Diego Choral Group. She directed the choir at St. Agnes Church for six years.

We performed at the dedication ceremonies of the restoration of Mission San Diego de Alcalá, in 1934. Doc Stewart played the organ and we sang one of his compositions. Mr. Thill was the director. Doc Stewart was one of San Diego's famous musicians. His real name was Dr. Humphrey John Stewart. He was the first city organist here. John D. Spreckels employed him to play the outdoor organ in Balboa Park. This organ was given to the city by Mr. Spreckels. He loved the organ. He had organs everywhere he went, and he played them all. Doc Stewart was mayor of Coronado at one time. He wrote many musical compositions and was commended by the pope for his achievements.

We sang with Dr. Earl Rosenberg, another well known San

Diego conductor. He directed a chorus of 500 voices during the 1935 exposition here. Madame Ernestine Schuman-Heinke was the soloist. (She was a famous German singer who became an American citizen and lived here in Coronado and in Grossmont.) We were in many Portuguese singing groups, also, my wife and I.

We were married, oh, gosh, almost ten years when we bought our first car. We had Richard and Doris and were living in the house on Thirty-second Street. We bought a second-hand Studebaker.

The first new car we bought was a Star—a Durant Star, with a four cylinder red-seal motor.

Later we had a Whippet. We called it the "Leaping Tuna." I took a trip to San Pedro in that thing, and when I got back I told Mary, "I'll never ride that darned thing again away from home because it whipped the devil out of me." Of course, the roads were not what they are today. On those rough roads that car would shake you to pieces.

From that, we went to a family car, a Willys Knight. That's another car that we could never forget. I drove it downtown one day. While I went in the gas company (San Diego Gas and Electric Company) I left it parked in the street. The key was in the car all the time. You never took the key off. Everyone trusted everyone else in those days.

I came out of the gas company, jumped in the car and took off, going down Broadway to our place of business, which was at the foot of E Street.

I got clear to Third and Broadway—the gas company was on Sixth Street—before I looked around and said to myself, "My God, this is not my car!" I rushed back. Thank God, the parking place was still open! I parked the car there and picked up mine, which was nearby. I left. Nobody seemed to notice anything.

One night, several weeks later, another event occurred concerning that car. I took my family to a show. While they were there, I went to the Elk's Club. The Chanters were doing some singing. I was in full dress.

We left the car on C Street. I was to meet Mary at the time we figured she would get out of the show. We both arrived, but there was no car. I wanted to report it to the police, but I didn't remember the license number. We came home by taxi. I went from there to the police department and, in full dress, made a report.

Three or four days later, the Los Angeles police found the car. It was parked on a side street. They picked it up because it was overparked. When they took it to a garage, they found it was stolen. The motor wasn't damaged. The only thing that was damaged was the cloth lining between the two sets of seats. Apparently the thieves had something solid, probably an iron safe, between the seats, and the safe cut the cloth that was against the back of the front seats.

We had insurance on the car. A fellow by the name of Stewart Kendall handled it. I think the company was Hartford. He had offices in the Spreckels Theater Building.

Before Prohibition—the Volstead Act—I made wine every year. All the Portuguese did—and the Italians. We'd make sixty or a hundred gallons. We gave it as presents or used it at family functions. After the country went dry, I didn't make any more. I had about one hundred gallons left which I stored away, to make it last. I had a place fixed in my laundry room in our house —like a cupboard, where I put the wine.

Once in a while, when we had a use for wine, we'd take some. One day when I went to get wine, I noticed matches and cigarette stubs scattered on the floor.

I thought, "Oh, oh, somebody's been here." I looked around and measured the contents of the barrels. Most of our wine was gone.

I went downtown and bought an alarm system. We connected it to the closet door where the wine was kept. The bell would ring in our bedroom. I never owned a gun up to that time, but my father-in-law had one. When he owned the saloon he used the gun for protection when he took his money home at night. He had no saloon at that time; so I went down—we all went down—to my father-in-law's house. I borrowed his gun. It was a revolver. We reached home about eleven o'clock, more or less, and put the children to bed. We got in bed ourselves. We hadn't been in bed but ten minutes when the buzzer started to ring.

"Oh, oh," I said, while getting up.

I put on a bathrobe and walked to the back door. We had many big trees in the yard. It was dark. I didn't dare go there, for I had no idea whom I might encounter. Instead, I went around the front of the house and to the side.

I had instructed Mary to call the police. I stood near the alley that came through behind our property. I didn't go out in the open. I waited until I heard people come out of the laundry room. When I figured that they were close, I jumped into the middle of the alley and I said, "Put up your hands or I'll fill you full of lead!"

All you could hear was bottles dropping. The thieves had wine jugs which they dropped when they put up their hands. Their pockets were filled with fruit jars—our fruit jars—we kept them in that cupboard. The fruit jars were filled with wine. The thieves were trying to hold them in their pockets. They dropped, too.

A car was parked on the other side of the alley, but I didn't go to the car, which is what I should have done. As I said, they came out with their hands up. I told them, "Get down underneath the archway light. I want to see what you sons-of-guns look like." (I might have used some stronger language, I don't recall for sure.)

There were three youngsters. I didn't know one from another. I'd never seen them before. Pretty soon the police car came. The policeman asked, "What's the trouble?"

"I caught these guys trespassing on my property. They stole some wine."

"All right, we'll take them to the jail. You come down in the morning, and we'll prefer charges."

Mary and I went back to bed. We weren't in bed more than ten minutes when the darn bell started ringing again. I had informed the police that there was a car back near the alley, but when they went to see to whom it was registered, the car was gone. I told Mary that someone had been waiting in the car for the others; that he had gone to get some more people, and had returned, maybe armed. I asked her to call the police. "What, again?" asked the police.

I stood at the front door, where I could hear the buzzer. It stopped when the intruders closed the door to the laundry room. I thought we had them, but the police car came down the street, its siren blowing to beat the devil! The thieves ran out, got in the car and drove out in the street. The police came up right then. "There they go!" I said. The police followed them. They traveled about two blocks, to where there was a jog in the street. They had to slow down, and the police caught them. There were five people in a pickup truck and a barrel with sediment in the bottom. The police told me to come down in the morning and prefer charges against them, also.

When I went down the next morning the police brought them all in and lined them up in front of the judge. His name was Chambers. They all pleaded guilty, of course. None had a dime. The judge fined them twenty-five dollars each, and gave them two weeks to pay the fine. I left.

Pretty soon a policeman came after me. "Mr. Oliver," he said, "the judge wants to see you."

"What the devil does he want?" I asked. After all, I'd had no sleep and my morning ruined.

"I don't know," replied the policeman. "He wants to see you."

I went back to the courtroom. The judge said, "Mr. Oliver, I am going to fine you fifty dollars for having wine in your possession."

I didn't say anything. I was thinking, but I didn't say anything. It doesn't pay. I paid the fifty dollars and walked away —but that's not the end of the story.

I was anxious to know where the thieves obtained the information that I had the wine. There was only one person besides my own relatives who knew about it. He was an employee; he was like one of the family. He had helped me to build the cupboards. When we had the sick baby, his wife helped Mary to nurse her.

Afterward he had some personal problems come up. There was a strain between us. I tried to help him, but this didn't work out. I had to let him go. I had it in my mind that he had something to do with this incident and I wanted to know whether this assumption was correct. A friend advised me to go see a clairvoyant. I never believed in clairvoyants, but it only cost a dollar. I said to myself, "I'm going to try it."

I went to this man and paid him a dollar. He said, "You want some information. You've got some kind of business close to the waterfront that grinds. I can see it turn. It grinds."

"That's the ice crusher," I said to myself.

(This man didn't know me at all.) He went on, "I can see a man who wears very heavy glasses. He looks as though he were German."

That's all I got for my dollar, but I felt satisfied. I knew that the man whom the clairvoyant described was the same man who worked for me and whom I had let go.

I never did anything about it. Later on, many years later on, he came to me and apologized and begged my forgiveness for all the trouble he had caused me. He passed away not too long after that.

Chapter XIV

Growing Civic Stature

In 1929, my wife and I bought a lot in Point Loma, on which we eventually built our permanent home. I don't believe that any lot on the hill surpasses ours for the view. From it you can see the harbor, the city of San Diego, Mexico, and the mountains toward the east. We were anxious to build a nice house, but the depression came along, and we decided to wait.

That depression was bad. It seemed as though every day someone came to see me at the plant, asking for a job, asking if I knew where he could get a job. I did everything that I could for these men. I found jobs for many of them. Usually, when they came to see me, I gave them a few dollars to tide them over while I looked for something for them. I knew what it was like to be "low on luck," as the saying goes.

It was not until 1934 that we started construction of our home on Point Loma. Frank Hope, one of San Diego's fine architects, designed our home. We moved in during the month of June, 1935. "We were in love with the place and still are in love with it. There isn't a thing we would change, even now," my wife has declared.

Mary kept asking the architect, "Are you sure it's big enough? Are you sure it's big enough?" That was her one big worry.

She explained, "We had lived in the house on Thirty-second Street and other places where the rooms were so small that every time I wanted to clean a room I had to shove all of the furniture out in the hallway. I had bruised hips and shins for years from falling over furniture. That's why I kept asking, 'Are you sure it's big enough?' "

121

He'd answer, "Well, Mrs. Oliver, I really think the house is big enough."

Our home in Point Loma, as seen from the air, soon after we built it in 1936. The house is centered in the picture.

Our home, from the bay side.

When they started putting it up, I looked it over and said, "Big enough it is." It has been, all right. Mary likes the place because we raised the family here and when we have them and all the grandchildren back there is room for everyone.

After we built the home on Point Loma, we became more and more involved in community affairs. We entertained many people in our home over the years, family and friends, and all types of dignitaries.

I found myself doing a good deal for the Portuguese who came here to settle or for those who came from out of town to visit. I took them here. I took them there. I interpreted for them. I took them to the doctor and the lawyer and the bank. I tried to help them find jobs and places to live. When the Portuguese and Brazilian dignitaries came to San Diego, the city had us on call to entertain them. I spent many hours doing that— and so did my wife; so did other Portuguese people.

I, also, found myself receiving invitations to join civic groups and to serve as an officer and on the board of directors of several. I was asked to participate in many fund-raising campaigns for worthy causes. I was glad to help. I wanted to do anything I could for this country and for its people, both of which had been very good to me—and for the town, which now was my town.

I joined the Chamber of Commerce and became a director. I was a director for from four to six years.

I was in the Elks, but active only in the Chanters, the singing group. I belonged to the Symphony Association—I should say we belonged—and to the Foresters of America; the Optimists; the Rotary Club; the Downtown Business Men's Association; and the American Tuna Boat Association. I was a director there for a while. Mrs. Belle Benchley, the woman director of the San Diego Zoo, appointed me to its board. We worked hard to raise money for the zoo in those days. I was a director of the San Diego Athletic Club for some time and a director of the Red Cross. I was on the Chamber's Harbor Committee and belonged to the San Diego Employer's Association.

In 1933 a man named C. Arnholt Smith bought out the interests of the U.S. National Bank in San Diego, a bank which had been chartered in 1913.

He had come here as a young boy from the town of Walla Walla, Washington, with his family. He quit school when he was sixteen and went to work for a man named Milton Heller, who had opened a grocery store at Eleventh and F Streets in 1892. His second job was with the Bank of Italy, which had started out as Merchant's National Bank. Bank of Italy later became the Bank of America. By the time he acquired U.S. National Bank, Mr. Smith had become a vice-president of the Bank of America.

When he bought the bank, I went in as a director. This was in August of 1934. I had no connection with him before he bought the bank. I bought a few shares of stock, but I wasn't even a depositor when he took over. A boy I knew, a young man, he was Portuguese, worked there. He asked me to move my account into the bank, which I did. His name was John Athaide. He's now a vice-president. Mr. Smith has said that I was one of the first accounts to move in after he bought the bank. I had traded with Bank of America when he worked there, but I never met him until I was asked to become a director.

The bank was very small then. Melvin N. Wilson was president, L. G. Purna was a vice-president and so was Mr. Smith. Jim Pfanstiel, who was my attorney, was a member of the board, as was Judge Gordon Thompson, Senior.

I was a director from 1934 to 1971. When I retired, I was given a solid silver plaque. It states, "The Board of Directors of the U.S. National Bank, on this day, March 16, 1971, in recognition of his devotion to duty and inestimable contributions, do confer the title of 'Director Emeritus' upon Lawrence Oliver, Director, 1934-1971."

At the time that I was appointed to the board of directors of the bank, I received a note of congratulations from Pete W.

Ross, who had been the principal of the Middletown School, when I was a pupil there, after I first came to San Diego.

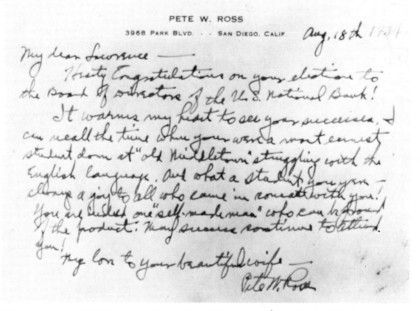

PETE W. ROSS

3968 PARK BLVD. - - SAN DIEGO, CALIF.

This is the note which I received from Pete W. Ross, my former principal at Middletown School, when I was appointed to the board of directors of the U.S. National Bank.

"My dear Lawrence,

"Heary Congratulations on your election to the Board of Directors of the U.S. National Bank!

"It warms my heart to see your successes. I can recall the time when you were a most earnest student down at 'old Middletown' struggling with the English language. And what a student you were—always a joy to all who came in contact with you! You are indeed one 'self-made man' who can be proud of the product. May success continue to attend you!

"My love to your beautiful wife,

Pete W. Ross"

(He was a man dedicated to his work and sincerely fond of his students. He never forgot a pupil. He was a source of inspiration to me, and to many other pupils.)

One of the bad loans on the books when Mr. Smith took over the bank was one made out to National Iron Works. Mr. Smith acquired National Iron Works, renamed it National Steel and Shipbuilding Corporation and began building and repairing tuna clippers. He sold the firm, I believe, in 1957.

125

One day in January, 1947, I was sitting in my office when my secretary came in and said, "There are two gentlemen here to see you."

"Show them in," I told her.

When they came in, they were Laurie Klauber, he was vice-president of the San Diego Gas and Electric Company at that time, and Oakley Hall, who was the owner of the San Diego Marine Construction Company, where I had some boats built. Mr. Klauber I had never met, although his family, of the Klauber-Wangenheim Company, was prominent here in town, and he was known even then as an expert on rattlesnakes. In my opinion, he was one of the most brilliant men the company ever had. I served with him on the board of directors of the zoo, also.

When I saw them come in, I said to myself, "I'm in for something," for I was always being asked to donate to some worthy cause or to be part of a committee to raise money for some charity. I never could say no.

I asked, "Gentlemen, what am I indebted to you for in this visit?"

Mr. Klauber replied, "Take your hand out of your pocket. We are not going to ask for any donations. We have come here to ask you to join our board of directors."

His remarks came as a real surprise to me. Although at one time I was considered the largest single shareowner of stock in the company, still I felt that this type of business was out of my field of experience.

I responded, "Mr. Klauber, what do I know about the San Diego Gas and Electric Company business—nothing, absolutely nothing."

He told me, "You don't have to know. We have people to run our business. You are a businessman. You know business principles. You are well known in this town. You have many friends. You have a reputation for being an honest businessman, and that's the type of man that we like to have on our board of directors."

"I will let you know in a few days. I must think this over," I answered.

"Fine," they replied.

I came home, and I talked the matter over with my wife. I told her that I didn't think that I belonged with a group like that—they all were professional men, well educated men, and I knew nothing of running a utility. She commented that she thought it would be a challenge and would give me prestige. She said that maybe they wanted a different type of man with a different background on their board.

With my wife's encouragement, I decided to accept the offer. In a day or two I called and told the company that I would accept. I stayed there eighteen years, until I was seventy-eight years old. While on the board, I voted for a resolution which would retire directors after they were seventy-two, but in the

When I retired from the board of directors of the San Diego Gas and Electric Company, two other members retired with me. They were Lawrence Klauber, at the extreme right, and Bernard W. Lynch, next to him. Mr. Klauber was a past president of the company and chairman of the board. He was one of the two men who called on me to ask me to join the board. As I mentioned in this book, I had great admiration for him, both as a man and as an executive. The man presenting us with these awards was Walter Zitlau, who then was an executive vice president of the firm. He was going on the board at that time. Today he is the president of the company. I always felt that he, too, was a very capable man.

process of getting the board adjusted to this I was requested to stay on until I was seventy-five. I appreciated the association with these men on the board and the fellowship which I found there. They all were gentlemen, every one, and wonderful people. I enjoyed the work and seeing the company grow. I also, received a plaque from the San Diego Gas and Electric Company when I retired from its board.

Chapter XV

Portuguese Organizations, Fraternal And Civic

The Portuguese have always been great ones for working together and for keeping in touch with each other. This is especially true of the people of the Azores. As early as 1884, the Portuguese in California were printing newspapers. The first Portuguese newspaper in California was begun in San Francisco in that year. It was called the *Voz Portuguesa.*

A whole series of newspapers followed. Most of these have disappeared. I only know of two now being published. One is the *Voz de Portugal.* It comes from Hayward, California, three times a month. The other is *O Jornal Português,* which now is the oldest paper being published by the Portuguese in the state of California and the only weekly Portuguese paper in California. It is the result of an amalgamation of many Portuguese newspapers, beginning with *O Amigo dos Católicos,* founded in Irvington, California, in 1888. In 1896, the name was changed to *O Arauto.* It then was published from Oakland. In 1917, the paper was moved to San Francisco and its name became *O Jornal de Notícias.* In 1932, it was amalgamated with two other papers, *Imparcial,* founded in Sacramento in 1903, and *Colónia Portuguesa,* begun in 1924, but I don't know where. It has been published from Oakland under the title of *O Jornal Português,* ever since.

As soon as they were in California—and this happened in other places, too—the Portuguese started forming societies in order to help themselves. These people, when they first came to California, were very poor. If someone took sick, if he died, there was no money to take care of the emergency. At first, the people took up collections among themselves. They never asked for anything from anyone else. This is not their nature. It is their nature to depend on themselves. Out of this habit grew their fraternal organizations. The idea behind them was protection. The people got together. They paid dues every month. When anybody passed away, or there was sickness, benefits came. Later, new ideas entered into the organizations. Today, the fraternal organizations sell all types of insurance policies, endowment, pay-life, and so on. They are regulated by the Insurance Commission.

From what I understand, the first protective society was formed on August 6, 1868 in San Francisco. It was the *Associação Portuguesa Protectora e Beneficiente*. The *União Portuguesa do Estado da Califórnia* was formed in San Leandro, on August 1, 1880; the *Irmandade do Divino Espírito Santo,* at San Jose Mission, on July 7, 1889; the *Sociedade Portuguesa Rainha Santa Izabel,* in Oakland, on March 15, 1898; the *Sociedade do Espírito Santo,* in Santa Clara, in 1895; the *União Portuguesa Protectora do Estado da Califórnia,* in Oakland, February 4, 1901; the *Associação Protectora União Madeirense do Estado da Califórnia,* in Oakland, 1913; the *União Portuguesa,* in 1916, which was succeeded by the *União Portuguesa Continental do Estado da Califórnia,* in Oakland, October 11, 1917; and the *Irmandade de Santa Maria Madalena,* in Oakland, July 26, 1930.

Out of all these groups there are about seven left. They are the *Associação Protectora União Madeirense do Estado da Califórnia;* the *Irmandade do Divino Espírito Santo;* the *Sociedade do Espírito Santo;* the *Sociedade Portuguesa Rainha Santa Izabel;* the *União Portuguesa do Estado da Califórnia;* the *União Portuguesa Protectora do Estado da Califórnia;* and the *Associação Portuguesa Protectora e Beneficiente,* which changed its name, in August 1948, to the Benevolent Society of California. In 1957, it affiliated with *União Portuguesa Continental do Estado da Califórnia.* Together they formed a new corporation, known as United National Life Insurance Society.

I joined two fraternal organizations and was quite active in both of them. They were the *Irmandade do Divino Espírito Santo* and the *União Portuguesa do Estado da Califórnia.*

I became a member of the *Irmandade* on February 15, 1914, shortly before my Naval Reserve unit was sent to the border. I was a delegate to the convention of the *Irmandade* when Mary and I went on our honeymoon, in October 1915. *Irmandade* means brotherhood; so the society is the Brotherhood of the Divine Holy Spirit. It is a statewide organization and a very large one.

I served from outside guard to master of ceremonies, which is going from the lowest to almost the highest position. The next step for me was the vice-presidency and the presidency. This was in the 1930's. I disliked doing it, but at this point I withdrew. I had worked hard to rise in rank in the local council; but advancing would mean that I must leave my family and my business for a year while traveling to the different councils in all the major cities of California. I would be on call anywhere in the state, any time, all during the year. I didn't feel that I could afford to give that much time to the organization.

The other society which I joined was the *União Portuguesa do Estado da Califórnia,* or the Portuguese Union of California. I became a member on April 15, 1917. This is the same type of organization as the *Irmandade,* only, I believe, larger—at least it was then.

I was the president, and I was the secretary here and was a delegate to the convention many times. In October, 1939, I was elected Supreme Director of the Union. It had eight to ten thousand members at that time. I served as Supreme Director for four years.

As Supreme Director, my duties were primarily connected with business and with people in need. I went once a month to San Leandro, California, to attend the directors' meetings. The union owned its own building there. We invested money, paid benefits, and so on. It was the responsibility of the directors to look for new methods and for devices which would help to serve the people and to improve the organization.

After I served as Supreme Director for four years, I declined to serve again, although I enjoyed the lodge and went through all the chairs in the local council.

In 1939, that same year in which I was elected Supreme Director, I was honored by my friends and relatives with a banquet in the El Cortez Hotel. This was in December. The program consisted of: Master of Ceremonies, M. E. Simas; Speakers, Right Rev. Lawrence Forrestal, Councilman Fred W. Simpson, Professor M. S. Cardoza, Judge Gordon Thompson, Junior, Frank Rodricks, and D. R. Minshal; Entertainment, Norman Oliver, Edward Cramer, Mary Delores Verrissimo, Ludres Sousa, Mary Balelo, Evelyn Medina, Delores Paixão, Point Loma Drill Team; Soloists, Mrs. Evelyn M. Glover, and Mrs. Mary Medina.

My wife belongs to two Portuguese women's fraternal organizations. They are the *Sociedade Portuguesa Rainha Santa Izabel,* or the Society of Queen Saint Isabel, and the *União Portuguesa Protectora do Estado da Califórnia,* or the Portuguese Protective Society of the State of California.

The men's fraternal groups are much older than those formed by the women. My wife tells me that the Society of Queen Saint Isabel was founded at the foot of the altar of a church called Saint Joseph's, in Oakland. Thirty ladies were present to form that group. (Queen Saint Isabel has quite a history, which I will discuss more thoroughly later on.)

There was no council, or branch in the San Diego area until June 12, 1913. At that time Council Number 98 was founded through the instigation of a Portuguese lady here named Mrs. Perpetua Soares. She worked with a lady from northern California who was named Mrs. Eugenia Rose Garcia. The council was called Saint Eugenia after her. The ceremony was conducted by the Supreme President, Maria Adelaide B. Encarnacão (Soares).

My wife was present and so was her mother. It had as charter officers: Ex-President, Maria Brown Soares; President, Laura da Conceição Soares; Vice-President, Perpetua Viera Soares; Secretary, Maria Emília Medeiros; Treasurer, Isabel Josephine Soares; Marshal, Conceição Monise; Guard Helen Goulart; Directors, Maria L. Monteiro, Elena Goulart, and Emerenciana Miller.

Other ladies present, according to my wife, were: Maria J. Medina, Maria Rita Machado, Rita Correia Silva, Rita Monise, Mary V. Medina, Adela Stanton, Angela Lawrence, Adelaide Silveira, Maria A. Goulart, Florinda Candida Soares, Mary Rosa Goulart, Maria Soares, Filomena George, and Maria Rita Monteiro.

Mary's mother and her aunts and most of the women in her family were interested in the formation of this society. It was a way of getting the women together. At the beginning of the Portuguese community here, the women had no contact except through the family. There were so few Portuguese at first that it didn't matter. Everyone knew everyone else, but as the community grew, there grew a need to bring Portuguese women together. The organizations gave them a chance to get out, to meet other ladies, to do charitable work, and to learn how to handle the problems and wants which they had experienced separately. Later, when they attended conventions in other parts of the state, they became acquainted with Portuguese women throughout California.

Portuguese women venerate Queen Saint Isabel, and in this society they try to follow her three virtues: charity, faith, and humility.

On May 23, 1922, a second council was formed in the San Diego area. This was Council Number 123, founded chiefly by Mary's mother, Emerenciana Miller, her aunts, Euzebia Soares and Angela Lawrence, and Mary herself. The Supreme President, Senhorinha E. Simas, of Oakland, organized the council. Twenty charter members were installed on that day.

Mary served as Grand President of the entire organization during the year, 1946-1947. At that time it was the largest women's group in the state of California. Whether it still is, I don't know.

In 1948, she was one of the very few members of the organization to be privileged to attend mass in the chapel of the Convent of Santa Clara Velha, in Coimbra, Portugal. Queen Saint Isabel often attended mass in this chapel. Her casket, which is made of crystal and silver, reposes there.

The Grand Council, Grand Officers and members of all councils in California donated three rose windows for the chapel. A total of twenty-eight members of the society were present, including Anna Veira, Past Grand President, and my wife, also a Past Grand President. John Valim, who was then the Grand Secretary of the United Portuguese of the State of California, delivered an address.

After the mass, the statue of Queen Saint Isabel was carried across the river Mondego into the city of Coimbra. As it passed under the arch of the bridge which spans the river, brilliant fireworks exploded. Her statue was on display in a church until the following day.

Council Number 123, the second council to be formed here, in May, 1972, celebrated its fiftieth anniversary. My wife, who is the only living founding member, was the guest of honor. She presented the council with a gold trimmed booklet, containing a history of the council, which she had written.

My wife joined the Portuguese Protective Society in the 1930's. She has been a member for many years. It has two councils here.

Mary has explained often to people that: "None of these fraternal organizations has ever tried to exert any political influence, neither the men's groups or the women's. We could demonstrate a good deal of strength and influence if we wanted to do this, for there are thousands of people involved in the Portuguese fraternal groups. This is not our purpose. Basically, what we want to do is to help each other with our mutual problems, and to grow to be better citizens, assisting our country.

"We, also, want to try to preserve the things that are Portuguese. As we have said, the Portuguese have a philosophy of trying to do things for themselves, by themselves. We vie among each other for the honor of doing the best job. The Portuguese are never jealous of anything which other members of the community might possess or achieve. We always figure that if we want it, too, we'll find a way to get it; but, if one Portuguese outdoes another—he builds a bigger boat, or has a bigger home, or does more for the community, that's a different story. You'll see the fellow who's been outdone really go to work."

In the course of our work within the local Portuguese community, Mary and I, along with many other Portuguese in the area, were in a position to see the community needs of our people. As a result of these observations, two local Portuguese groups were formed.

The Portuguese-American League was begun in 1936. This group represents all of the Portuguese-American organizations in San Diego. It raises funds to entertain dignitaries from out of town. It sprang from the California Pacific Exposition of 1935-1936.

During the exposition, we maintained the House of Portugal in the House of Pacific Relations. This was a special area, set apart to represent all nations. I was chairman, and Mary was in charge of the house and the hostesses. The women furnished the house with authentic Portuguese furniture, lent to us by Dr. Carlos Fernandes, a medical doctor in San Francisco. These articles he had imported from Portugal.

They obtained special curtains embroidered as they would be in Portugal. They fixed showcases with all of the fancy Portuguese crochet and other needlework done in silver—and what all else they had, I don't remember. The women kept the house open every day. For two years we had charge of that house. Then the interest died away.

On September 29, 1935, the league sponsored a Portuguese Day at the exposition. We invited Doctor João Antonio de Bianchi, the Minister of Portugal in Washington, D.C., to be our guest, along with his wife, Madame de Bianchi. They accepted. We presented a program put on by Portuguese people from all over the state, portraying different customs and dances of native Portugal.

The women had a man come down from San Francisco, a Mr. Carvalho, especially to teach the dances. There they ran into a problem. The boys wouldn't participate. They refused to dance. "So," as Mary said, "we had no other choice. We had to use the girls, dressed as boys, to dance. At Coimbra, the great University of Portugal, (which was founded in 1290, in Lisboa, during the reign of the king, Dom Diniz, and Queen Isabel) the boys wear long black capes which they use in different manners. Each gesture is significant. They throw them around their shoulders. They throw them around their heads. When they serenade the girls at night with their guitars, they partially cover their faces with their capes. I understand that every niche in the capes meant a romantic conquest, so the more ragged the capes, the more admired the man.

"We taught the girls to use the capes, and when the Minister of Portugal came to San Diego, the girls swept their capes to one side; so he walked through the center of the group. He was thrilled, very thrilled. The ceremony brought moisture to his eyes. It was as though he were in his own country.

"We also put on a show of the capes for the children at Cabrillo School, which was opened long before we moved to Point Loma, 1921, if I remember correctly. Their principal, Harold S. Kimball, and his wife, brought the children."

Mary had another unusual experience when the Minister came. We held a large banquet at the El Cortez Hotel, and we invited the city officials and dignitaries from all over California. We really put on a show. Like all Portuguese, the Minister was crazy for fish and for fishing. The next day we chartered a sport fishing boat. We took him and his wife, plus a few other dignitaries from out of the city, on a fishing trip over to the Coronado Islands. The day was beautiful. Everyone had a good time. The Minister was extremely happy. He caught many fish, yellowtail, bonita, barracuda, and bass. His wife loved fishing, also. She really enjoyed herself.

The next day Mary had a big job. She spent the day in the house, "cooking all that fish. We had invited a few friends to have dinner with us and with the Minister and his wife. He said to me, 'Will you make a *caldeirada*?' I asked myself, 'What in the heck is a *caldeirada*?' To him I replied, 'Tell me how to do it, and I'll be happy to make it for you.'"

That's where Mary ran into the problem. He didn't know how to make that dish. You see, he was of English extraction, born on the island of Madeira, which made him a Portuguese subject. He was educated at Oxford. His wife was of no help either, for she was of Russian extraction.

He said to Mary, "Well, forget it, forget it." Mary couldn't forget it. If someone whom she knows wants something, she's going to get it for him. She asked me about it, but they don't make *caldeiradas* where I come from. It's strictly a Madeira dish. Mary learned her Portuguese cooking from her mother; so that was no help.

My wife went around asking everyone she could think of, "How do you make a *caldeirada?*" Most of them answered, "Make a what—never heard of it."

Finally someone gave her a recipe. I don't know who was the happier, Mary or the Minister and his wife. She found out as she remarked, "that it is a stewed fish with a delicious gravy. You put bread on the bottom of the fish dish and put the stewed fish and potatoes over it. I had fried fish. I had baked fish. I had broiled fish. I had fish in every manner I could think of, with sauces that came from Portugal and from the islands and from America. As the last entrée, I brought out a big platter of *caldeirada*. He and his wife were surprised and pleased. They ate and ate, as though they were family. 'This has been a great day,' he said. They were likeable people, very down-to-earth. That evening was quite a happy occasion. We have thought of it often."

Another thing that we noticed, was that the Portuguese colony here in the San Diego area got together only once a year—when we had the celebration of the Pentecost. Afterward, everybody scattered, unless there was a benefit or some other special occasion. It seemed to me and to some others that what we needed was a social and civic club where we could get together regularly, renew our friendships, keep the Portuguese culture alive, and do something for ourselves and for the good of the community as a whole.

We organized the Portuguese-American Social and Civic Club on December 15, 1940, with approximately 125 members. I was the first president. M. O. Medina was vice-president. M. M. Frizado was secretary and Mrs. Minnie Cardoza was treasurer.

When the club was organized, I made an inaugural speech in Portuguese in which I set down the goals of the group.

What I said was that we were a hard working and honorable people, but that there was little communication between us, as a people, and our community. Therefore we wanted to form a club, as other groups had done already. We wanted this club to show the world what we are and to represent us in community activities. We, also, wanted it to give us and our families entertainment and recreation and wanted it to assist us with preserving the Portuguese traditions; but, I pointed out, we couldn't help ourselves or our country if we didn't have unity. This the club would give us.

I ended by wishing everyone a Merry Christmas and a Happy New Year.

> *"Muito obrigado.*
> *"Portugueses, meus amigos.*
> *"Naturalmente a apresentação que*

138

acabastes de ouvir, foi um tanto quanto exageráda.

"Mas, como Portugueses que me prezo de ser, não poderia recusarme a tomar parte em tudo quanto nos honre e dignifique.

"Nós temos sido um povo honrado e trabalhador; mas sobre o ponto de vista cívico, temos muito acabados segundo outras colonias deste Estado. Naturalmente alguns de vós já perceberam, que para haver força cívica necessita-se estar organizados para podermos exijir o que nos é devido.

"E como nos podemos organizar? Por meio da formação dum clube, que, nem só nos dará direitos cívicos, mas bem assim sociais e recriativos. Sociais, para podermos mostrar aos estrangeiros que somos unidos. Recriativo, para nosso entertenimento, e de nossas familias. Mas sem nos juntarmos nada se consegue; eis a razão porque hoje comemorando o dia do Natal, a e ao mesmo tempo aproveitar-se-á ocasião para angariar membros para dar início a formação dum clube.

tenho dito

"A TODOS DESEJO UMAS BOAS FESTAS DO NATAL, E UM FELIZ ANO NOVO."

Both Mary and I belonged to the Portuguese-American Social and Civic Club for over twenty years. We served as officers many times. The group meets once a month. It has a social. It takes part in civic affairs, representing the Portuguese.

It uses Portuguese foods and dances. It tries to keep up the old traditions. Use of the Portuguese language was required at first, but that requirement was changed. The meetings now are conducted in English, to my sorrow.

Here a group of members of the Portuguese-American Social and Civic Club were dressed for a masquerade party, held in 1954. The four people in front are Tony and Edna Madruga, Deutilde Varley and Arnold Neves. In the rear are Aurora Goma, Machado Medina, Maria Rita and Tony Rosa, Marcella and Juaquin Theodore, Mary and Tony Monise, Doris and myself, her uncle, Dennis Oliver, and his wife, Laura.

Our son, Richard, and his family. Richard and his wife, De Von are in front. Lawrence Richard, or Rick, Marie Leilane, and Thomas Patrick are in the rear.

Norman Oliver, with his children, Renée Dolores, Mark Lawrence, and Stephen Lawrence.

Our daughter, Doris Oliver Porto, with her son, Joseph Oliver, next to her in the top row and Andrew, or Drew Oliver, with Christopher Oliver at his left, in the the bottom row.

Mary and I when we were chairman of San Diego's last *Festa do Espíritu Santo,* in 1963. The *festas* involved a tremendous amount of work, but good times and wonderful memories resulted.

Our daughter, Doris Mary, wearing her wedding gown. Her mother searched the house but could not find a good picture of Doris as *festa* queen. Every woman looks especially nice on her wedding day. Doris was no exception.

Our granddaughter, Renée Dolores, when she was queen of the *Festa do Espíritu Santo*.

Our granddaughter, Marie Leilane, when she was queen of the *Festa do Espíritu Santo*.

Marie, kneeling at the altar. Three generations of Oliver women have been *festa* queens. My wife was the first, then Doris, our daughter, and later, our grand-daughters.

Chapter XVI

The Festa Do Espírito Santo

One of Portugal's most revered historical and religious figures is Queen Saint Isabel, the same person for whom the organization in which my wife has been so active was named. The queen was not a Portuguese by birth, however. She was the daughter of the king of Aragon. In 1279, when Portugal was ruled by the young monarch called *Diniz,* she was married to him. It was a political marriage.

The festivities went on for weeks. The young bride was charming and pretty, they say, but reserved and very religious. One day, she told the court that she had invited all of the poor of the community to be her guests at the palace. Furthermore, she was going to wash their feet and serve them bread and soup with her own hands. This dazed the court.

At first, her husband, as any new husband would, catered to her wishes, thinking that she would get over this deep interest in religion. He soon learned better. Instead of getting less religious, she grew more so. Her charities and her charitable performances kept growing. The court became concerned. The people went to the king and told him that the way she was spending on the poor meant that there would be nothing left for the court. Her husband grew displeased with her and refused her any more money for charity. That didn't stop her.

There are many legends regarding Queen Saint Isabel. One day, according to one legend, she saved bread from her own table to give to the hungry. She was sneaking out a side gate, with the bread concealed beneath her mantle, when she was stopped by the king. He demanded to know where she was going and what she had concealed under her cloak. After saying

141

a prayer, she threw open her cloak. Instead of bread, red roses tumbled out.

Another legend concerns the building of the Convent of Santa Clara Velha, in Coimbra, which was her idea. (This was where my wife was in 1948, at the mass.) After the convent was completed, the queen had no money to pay the workmen. Once again, she prayed for help. She was told in a dream to collect roses and to give them to the workmen. As the puzzled workmen took the roses from her hands, each rose turned into a bag of gold.

Another tale about Queen Saint Isabel has been responsible for one of the Portuguese people's most impressive religious celebrations, the *Festa do Espírito Santo,* or the Feast of the Holy Spirit.

(One thing I should make clear is that in referring to Portuguese celebrations, the word is *festa,* not *fiesta,* which is of Spanish derivation, although having the same meaning. It annoys the Portuguese to have their *festas* called *fiestas,* although most of the time they don't complain.)

So the story goes, at one time during her reign there was a terrible famine in Portugal. The queen depleted all her funds while seeking food for her people; she had no financial resources left, only her crown, the symbol of her royal state. One morning, at mass, she promised the Holy Spirit, "I will give my crown to the church if you will send me a miracle; so my people will be relieved of their hunger."

As she left the church, she saw ships coming into the harbor, loaded with wheat and corn! For over 700 years the Portuguese people have celebrated this event in the *Festa do Espírito Santo,* which commemorates the sainted queen and her miracle. (She was canonized in 1625 by Pope Urban VIII.) The *festa* features a parade and mass, followed by feasting, singing and dancing. There are big displays of fireworks. Each person is given a glass of wine and a piece of sweetbread, called *rusquilha.*

During the parade, a crown is carried to the church. This

represents the crown of the queen being offered to the church. Here in the United States, however, the Feast of the Pentecost has been modified to the extent that a queen is crowned during the festa. The queen represents Queen Saint Isabel.

Mary and I worked in the Feast of the Pentecost together for over forty years. She and her family worked in it before that.

The festa is not a church-sponsored activity, no more than a Saint Patrick's Day parade. Rather it is a religious celebration which is conducted by a little group known as the *Sociedade do Espírito Santo,* or Society of the Holy Spirit.

My wife recalls that San Diego's first real festa "was held in 1909 in La Playa, in a private building which had been made into a hall by the Portuguese people from La Playa and Roseville and San Diego. The festa was held there from 1909 to about 1914. When the owner of the lot wanted the land, the people had to move the building.

"In those early days we came over to the festa by ferry. The ferry left from the foot of Market Street. The slip on the Point Loma side was where the yacht club is now, at the foot of Talbot Street. We walked from the ferry slip into La Playa, which was just this side of Fort Rosecrans, the old army fort. La Playa means, the beach, by the way.

"The one who started the festas here was Frank Silva, a fisherman from the Cape Verde Islands. He was a good worker and a very religious man. He bought the crown for the queen; then he gathered the people together to pay for it and for all the other expenses, and to do the work involved. His daughter, Rose Silva, was the first queen of the festa here.

"Our church ceremony was held in the first little Saint Agnes Church in Roseville. The festival is held in May or June of every year.

"My mother and father were very hard workers in the early festas. In 1914, my uncle, Joe Lawrence, was the *mordome,* or chairman of the festa, and at that time I was the queen. This was the first festa held in the new hall, on Locust and Carleton

Streets, built by some Portuguese men. We held the festa there for five years.

The *Festa do Espíritu Santo* of 1914, in Point Loma. Mary's uncle, Joe Lawrence, was the mordome. Mary was the *festa* queen.

"There was always a big turnout. It was a family affair, held on Pentecost Sunday. During the first festas we walked from the ferry slip into La Playa and then on to Roseville, through the dust. The streets were unpaved for years after the festas were started. The ceremony would be held at the church. Afterward, we would walk back to La Playa for the dinner and the dancing. After the second hall was built, we walked five blocks to the hall and three blocks to the church. Sometimes we would miss the last ferry back to San Diego, and one of the fishermen would take us back into the city in his little boat. There was no street-car. No one had automobiles. Many times we walked up the boardwalk on Broadway late at night with our shoes in our hands, for we were tired from walking and dancing."

Until after Mary and I were married, I didn't participate in the festa. I attended, but I didn't take any active part. The first one I remember going to was around 1910. I became active after the split into two festas, one in San Diego and one in

144

Mary, as *festa* queen, in 1914. She was fifteen years old. It was in the spring of this same year, before I went to the border with my naval reserve unit, that I noticed that Mary no longer was only "a nice kid," and I asked her if I could call on her when I returned from my tour of duty with the Naval Reserves.

Point Loma. That was around 1920. From then on, there were two celebrations held each year, until 1963. During this time, I was very active and so was my wife.

The first chairman of the festa in San Diego was Harry Madruga, a brother of Manuel Madruga, Mary's godfather. I was the second mordome. The mordome goes around, starting in January, to the fishing boats, the canneries, all the Portuguese people, and the business houses which trade with the Portuguese, to ask for contributions of money and for articles to be raffled. In the evening of the festa, during the dancing intermissions, the mordome auctions off the gifts and raises more money.

The fishermen, by tradition, offered the Holy Spirit twenty-five cents a ton of their catch. Part of that went to the church and part to the festa. After the division into two festas became necessary, because of so many Portuguese people here, the giving of tonnage was stopped, on the San Diego side, at least.

With our first San Diego festa, we didn't raise any money. We went to Our Lady of Holy Angels Church. We had a small procession around the church and then went to Balboa Park, where we held a picnic.

After that, with my first chairmanship, we went to Our Lady of the Rosary Church, on Columbia and Date Streets. We had the ceremony there for about forty years. Our social, for a while, was held in the Knights of Columbus Hall on Fourth and Elm. Later, we moved it to the hall of Our Lady of the Rosary Church. Eventually the group attending grew so large that for many years we took over the Balboa Park Club.

When I had my first chairmanship, we had about fifty people attending. By the time we were having the social in the park, we were feeding fifteen hundred or more. These were Portuguese people and their friends. The crowds began getting bigger and bigger. This presented a problem, for the ceremony is a religious one. Many of the people who began to come were not interested in the religious aspect. We stopped a good deal of the publicity, thus restricting the activities pretty much to the Portuguese.

The new chairman, for the following year, begins his work a day or so after the celebration is over, when his election is held. He becomes responsible for all the financing. His wife has many responsibilities, also. In return for their work, the mordome and his wife are permitted to choose the queen. Our daughter, Doris, was queen twice. Both of our granddaughters, Marie and Renée, have been queens.

In the old country, it was the boys, not the girls, who had the honor of carrying the crown. Here it got started with the girls. I don't know why. Always in San Diego, though, we have had the queens. Maybe in other places in the United States the people once observed the ceremony in the same way in which it is done in the old country, but I have never seen it or heard of it.

I served as mordome about eight times. Each time, as with all mordomes, a heavy burden fell on my wife. Mary was responsible for all of the arrangements for the procession, the food, the hall, the publicity, the church decoration, the transportation, the costumes. She appointed the chairmen for these functions in January. She arranged for the children who would march in the procession. She was the diplomat, who smoothed over everything that went wrong.

"I selected every dress that was worn in the procession each time that Lawrence was mordome," my wife recalled recently. "Sometimes, a great many times, we bought the material and made the costumes, to carry out the theme of the procession. Each festa has its own theme. At the same time that I was in charge of the procession, I directed the choir, and I sang in the choir. We chose cooking crews. The women who cooked, worked for days ahead. They sometimes went all night without sleep. There were cleanup crews, who were up nearly all the night following the festa. We made special arrangements for the little children to be fed and for the old people and for the sick to get attention. It was quite a job. People don't want to work like that anymore."

In the early days, also, if the mordome happened to be the captain of a fishing boat, his boat was anchored below the hall in the harbor. It was decorated every night. He would have lights and fireworks. The crew wore special uniforms and marched in the procession. This is something else that we've lost. It was too expensive because the boat would lose a whole fishing trip. The fishing season starts around Easter. If the captain was mordome, he either had to keep his ship in port or hire another captain to take his boat out. The fishermen couldn't afford to do that. You see, in the old days, the celebration lasted from Thursday to Monday.

When San Diego had its last festa, in 1963, I was mordome and Mary, once again, worked with me. Nobody wants to work on the festas anymore, we learned. The young people don't care. The old ones are dying out, getting too old for the responsibility. It costs plenty. Everyone must donate and, also, those in the procession buy their own costumes. It takes several thousand dollars to put on a festa.

No one was interested in taking this last one; so I told my wife, "I know this is hard for us, but let's take it once more. Let's give a good one, but make it the last."

We didn't say anything to the people until the night of the festa. At that time we told them that this one was the last. The money that we had left over, we invested for the education of young priests at the University of San Diego. The revenue from the investment goes to the seminary.

We built a chapel in the Immaculata, the church at the University of San Diego. The second one from the left, as you go in, is ours. We put the crown in there, in a receptacle which I had built. The crown stands over the altar. That was the end of the festas in San Diego as far as we are concerned.

Chapter XVII

The Case Of The Kidnapped Statue

The Portuguese people always have been proud of the fact that it was João Rodriques Cabrilho, (Juan Rodriguez Cabrillo) a Portuguese working for Queen Isabella of Spain, who discovered San Diego, in 1542. Cabrillo National Monument, on the tip of Point Loma, commemorates this event. As I understand it, the monument attracts more visitors than any other national monument in the United States. One of its features is a statue of Cabrilho. It is fourteen feet high. It weighs 14,000 pounds and rests on a six ond one-half ton foundation. It is crowned by a shield bearing the Portuguese arms and above that the Christian cross.

San Diego almost didn't get that statue. In fact, we had to fight the rest of the state for it. I am pleased to have had a part in bringing it here, because here is where I have always thought it belonged.

In 1935, the Portuguese government authorized a Portuguese sculptor, Alvaro De Brêe, to begin work on a statue of Cabrilho, to be offered as a gift to the state of California; also it was to be exhibited at the exposition in New York in 1939. When it was completed, the statue was delivered to New York, but it never was exhibited there. It arrived too late, I heard.

As San Francisco was going to have an exposition in 1940, the statue was shipped there, to be placed on exhibit. As things turned out, it never was shown there, either.

I became involved in the affair of the statue in an indirect fashion. In March 1939, I received a letter from the secretary of the Committee of the House of Portugal. He was working on the arrangements to establish a House of Portugal in the expo-

Alvaro De Brêe. He was thirty-five years of age when he was commissioned by the government of Portugal to undertake the Cabrilho Statue. He came from a distinguished Portuguese family and was a student at the Fine Arts School of Lisboa.

sition grounds. The committee was asking for money through the different Portuguese groups to defray expenses for the House of Portugal. I proceeded to ask our people for money for that purpose.

When the money was ready to send, I wrote a letter to accompany it. I informed the committee that when the exposition was over, the people of Portuguese extraction in San Diego were requesting that the statue of Cabrilho be placed in San Diego. I explained that we felt it belonged here, from an historic and patriotic standpoint.

I waited for a long time for a reply. Finally, the secretary, J. C. Valim, wrote me a letter saying that the committee was in favor of placing the statue in San Diego. (This was the same John Valim who gave the speech at the chapel of Santa Clara Velha, in Portugal in 1948, several years later.) After that, I did not receive another word. I learned later that several other cities had requested the statue.

I waited until 1940, after the exposition was opened and I saw that the statue never appeared on the grounds. I spoke to different people whom I thought should know something, but no one seemed to know where it was—or anything about it.

I learned that the statue had come to California, but there was over $600.00 of duty on it, which the exposition committee did not pay. Instead, the committee gave the statue to the state, inasmuch as the state could get it out of customs without paying duty. The procedure was simple. The governor, Culbert Olson, accepted it. The statue was supposed to go to the Commissioner of State Parks, but we discovered that he never received it. We, also, learned that the governor had promised it to the people of Oakland, and that it had been hidden away.

When I found that it had been given to the state, I immediately contacted Col. Ed. Fletcher, who was then our state senator. (That term, colonel, was a nickname.) I felt that with his influence and prestige, plus his being in the legislature, he could do something, if anybody could. He was very gracious. He promised that he would do all he could for me and for the city of San Diego and its citizens.

On his next trip to Sacramento, he made some inquiries about the statue, but no one knew where it was. Upon his return, he

Our friend, Anna Lewis Miller, who had the Cabrilho Statue stored in her garage in San Francisco.

told me this. He said that if I could find it, he thought he could get it for San Diego. I replied that I would be glad to investigate further.

About thirty days later, my wife and I made a trip to Oakland and San Francisco. Once there, I made some inquiries among my friends concerning the statue; but still no one knew anything about it. It seemed that we were up against a blank wall. By a stroke of luck, my wife and I discovered where it was stored.

One day we went to San Francisco to visit a friend, Anna Lewis. (Her name is Miller now.) During the course of our conversation, the subject of the statue came up. Would we like to see it, she asked. Would we! It had been stored in her garage. Her husband, who had since passed away, had permitted the statue to be placed there. It never had been removed from the original box in which it had been shipped.

The garage where the Cabrilho Statue was hidden away.

I could hardly wait to get back to San Diego to tell Senator Fletcher about my find. He lost no time. "Leave it to me," he said. "We'll get it."

Immediately he obtained a permit to pick up the statue and to bring it to San Diego. One Saturday afternoon, when all

153

offices were closed, he went to our lady friend and presented the order to her. She was reluctant to turn the statue over to him, but it was Saturday afternoon. She could reach no one to help her. She felt that she must comply with the law.

Col. Fletcher had a truck with a crane. He took possession and delivered the statue to the Santa Fe Railway Station, with instructions to ship it out that night to San Diego. When the men moved it from the garage, they discovered that it had broken through the concrete in the floor. The statue, itself, was split through the middle. It was in parts; so the break did not matter too much.

On the following Monday, there was quite a turmoil around the bay area, in San Francisco and Oakland, when news of the "statue-snatching" got around. The committee went to Sacramento with its attorneys to try to get the governor to order the statue returned to San Francisco. He was in a spot because he had promised it to Oakland. Someone else had promised it to Sacramento, and Fresno thought that it should have it. The governor was upset and in a dilemma. I understand that in public he accused Senator Fletcher of stealing the statue, and threatened to invoke the law; but he never did anything.

When it arrived in San Diego, the statue was stored in the city shops, at Eighteenth and A Streets, while a site was being selected. It remained there until the city decided to have it placed near the water, facing the entrance to the bay, where the Sonar School is today.

Col. Fletcher and I had the statue repaired. When the grounds and platform were ready, we had it moved into place. I invited the Portuguese Consul General, Eculides Goulart da Costa, of San Francisco, to come to dedicate the statue. Our daughter, Doris, with two attendants, Lovela Duggin and Julia Brum, unveiled it at the ceremonies. A picture of Doris at the dedication is in the museum at Point Loma.

When World War II started, the government needed the area where the statue was situated, so it was moved to the tip of Point

Loma, near the lighthouse. Two Portuguese ships visited the bay in honor of the occasion. A ceremony was held, and representatives of the Portuguese government put up a plaque.

The dedication of the Cabrilho Statue, in 1940. The date was December 19. Lovela Duggin, my wife's second cousin, is at the extreme left. Doris, our daughter, is third, and to her left, Julia Brum, my niece, on my sister's side. The lady with the girls I cannot identify.

The Cabrilho Statue dedication, showing Joe Dryer, president of the San Diego Heaven on Earth Club, at the extreme right. He was a very active citizen and was involved in the struggle to bring the statue here.

Consul General of Portugal, Eculides Goulart de Costa, speaks at the dedication of the Cabrilho statue.

156

Later, in 1966, the government graded and landscaped a new spot. Today, the statue stands above the site where Cabrilho landed in 1542. For many years the story behind the statue was kept secret because of the hard feelings but that's all over now. The statue is where it belongs.

These people participated in the ceremony which was held when the Cabrillo Statue was moved to the tip of Point Loma, during World War II. The men in uniform are the Portuguese admirals, who brought their ships here. The lady who is third from the left is the wife of one of the admirals. The woman next to her is Mary Gigletto. Second from the left is the Portuguese Consul from Los Angeles, Joseph Segal. It was at this time that the plaque was put up.

A Cabrillo Day float from the city of Long Beach. This picture dates from the 1930s.

Chapter XVIII

Cattle, Camp Oliver, And Golf

After I bought my 2,200 acre ranch at Descanso, in 1942, I not only transferred the small herd of English Devon cattle which I had kept at the Camp Kearney ranch, but I increased my herd and developed an interesting and successful hobby of cattle-raising.

I started with the Devon and crossed them with what is called a White Face, but they did not make very good looking cattle; so I got rid of them and I went for White Face Herefords. These were beef stock. I had a roundup once a year and employed about four men on the ranch. I kept around 250 head on hand all the time. Then I went into purebred Herefords.

Soon I began showing my cattle. I showed at the first of the cattle season in Kansas City. From there, I went to Ogden, Utah, and on to Portland, Oregon. From Portland, we went to Los Angeles and San Francisco and then home. A few times I showed cattle in Phoenix.

Sometimes I made sales right during the show. I had an opportunity to sell an eighteen-month-old bull for $50,000, but I refused. That was during a show. I kept him for seven years. I sold one heifer, a daughter of this bull, for $12,000. He sired two reserve champions, that's a second place award, and he was a second place winner himself. The last year I showed cattle was 1956, when I had the undefeated heifer in the Pacific Northwest.

I owned the ranch from 1941 to 1958. I hated to sell it because I loved the place—we loved the place—and I enjoyed raising cattle; but I wasn't getting any younger. I went there

One of my prize yearlings from the Oliver Ranch

often to supervise. To Descanso was a long way at that time—
there were no freeways. Good help was hard to get.

We had built a beautiful ranch home there, which we used
on weekends. Our friends and our relatives came often. Our
children loved the ranch—and so did our grandchildren. Mary
was delighted with the opportunity of fixing up the house and
overseeing the landscaping. She remarked not long ago how she
felt: "I became interested in the cattle and enjoyed the cattle
shows. The cattle people are different and intriguing. I even
learned to ride a horse. Lawrence gave me a beautiful palomino
mare, but that one I never got to ride. Everyone told me, 'She's

My horse, Chief, and I. Chief stayed at the ranch when I sold it.

Some of my prize cattle, my pure bred Herefords.

too frisky for you. Wait until she's a little older.' I never did get to ride her. We called her 'April Gold.' When my son moved to Oregon, he took her there, to his ranch.

"We imported lilac from the east. We planted fruit trees and flowering trees and pines, which grew tall. The place was lovely. Our last day at the ranch was beautiful. It was the end of March. The new people were taking over on the first of April. I called the children to come out because the snow was falling and the scenery was gorgeous. Our daughter, Doris, was in Morocco at that time. Her husband was stationed there. The boys came, though, and brought their children.

"I was born in San Diego. I had never seen snow fall. The pines were covered. The bushes were blanketed. The ground was carpeted. The children made snowmen and snowballs. They were thrilled. It was a beautiful, beautiful day."

Still, at times I'm sorry that I sold that ranch. It gave us a good deal of pleasure. We had many happy days there. I don't feel as badly as I could, however, because of a project which evolved from our ownership of the property. My wife and I think that it is very worthwhile.

In the late 1940's, I heard that the Sisters of Social Service were looking for a place to build a camp for underprivileged children. I became interested in this undertaking, because I know something of the history of the organization. It is a Catholic religious community, founded in Hungary in 1908. The Sisters came to the United States in 1923 and to Los Angeles in 1926. Their Motherhouse, or headquarters, is in Los Angeles. The group came to San Diego in 1938.

Their main activity is social work. The Sisters try to help out in the community with whatever is needed. They try to be flexible and adaptable to changing conditions. They previously had established the Bayside Settlement in San Diego to assist the community.

I contacted the Sisters and invited them to come to see our place. They paid us a visit. We showed them the grounds. I asked them if they would like some of our ranch for their camp —could they use it—would it be appropriate?

Yes, they said, they liked it. They would love to have some of our land for their camp. In 1949, I gave them twenty-two acres of my ranch. Sister Katharine Salter was their director at that time. She made all the arrangements.

Groundbreaking took place in 1952. The camp was dedicated in 1954. The Sisters named it Camp Oliver, which was a surprise to me. They have a retreat there, where people go for quiet times, to think and talk, and a camp, which is used year-round. The Sisters try to incorporate something for all the age levels and for families.

Groundbreaking at Camp Oliver, in 1952. His Excellency, the Reverend Charles F. Buddy, is at my left. To his left is Sister Katharine Salter. The Sister to my right is Sister Frederica, who organized the Sisters of Social Service in the United States.

On May 28, 1972, the Sisters dedicated a new lodge, named for Sister Salter. She came down from Los Angeles for the ceremony. We had the pleasure of meeting once more. She is, as I am, over eighty years of age. She is more or less in retirement now.

The Juniors of Social Service assist with the financial responsibility for the camp. Each year they conduct the Mardi Gras Ball at the Hotel del Coronado. This ball raises funds to maintain Camp Oliver. The Juniors are a branch of the Social Service Auxiliary, an organization of women of the laity who assist the Sisters of Social Service in their work. The Sisters, and all of the women who help them, are hard-working and dedicated people.

Their camp is non-denominational. It handles 425 children each year and one-third of them are underprivileged. They attend on Camper-ships, from funds raised by the Juniors of the Social Service Auxiliary.

It is a continuing pleasure for my wife and for me to know that some of our former ranch is being used to bring happy and beneficial experiences to others, especially to children who otherwise might not have these opportunities. When I was a boy I was underprivileged also, but not in the same sense as the children today. I had plenty of room in which to play, but nothing to play with and no time for play. I remember what it feels like to be denied those wonderful free-and-easy days, to which, it seems to me, all children are entitled. It is my hope that Camp Oliver enriches the lives of all the people who come into contact with it. I know that it has enriched ours.

I traded the rest of the ranch for thirty-six apartments, which I sold in 1969.

In 1954, before I sold the ranch, I assumed part interest in the development of a golf course. Subsequently the Oliver family became the owners of the property.

The first time that I ever played golf was during the time when a friend of ours was manager of the Van Camp Sea Food Company. His name was Martin Quama. This was in the early 1930's. My wife and I and our family were going on our vacation, to Idylwild, in the San Jacinto mountains north of here. Mr. Quama was going to vacation at the same time at the same place. He told me, "Get a set of clubs and I'll show you how to play golf."

I bought a set of clubs and took them to let him show me how to play. That was a mistake. I should have taken some regular lessons. I tried to play after he showed me how to do it, but there were so many trees on that course that every time I played, it sounded as though a bunch of woodpeckers were there. I hit every tree—didn't miss one.

After I came back to San Diego, I joined the San Diego Country Club and took some lessons from a well known pro here, Fred Sherman.

I played once a week, on Saturdays, usually. The businesses were operating smoothly. I spent less time at the plant. Particularly after my son, Richard, came to work for me, things were much easier. I was relieved of a great deal of responsibility for the plant. By the late 1930's, I considered myself more or less retired from it.

World War II came. I had a steam engineer's license. Help was hard to get. It was necessary to run the factory night and day. I took the night shift, running the boilers and the equipment. Richard operated them during the day.

At that time I was forced to abandon golf. I didn't have the time. Later on, with the war over, I bought a membership in the Mission Valley Country Club. I played a little. I never kept score. I went mainly for the fellowship and the fresh air and exercise.

In 1954, I bought an interest in the golf course which we now own. Sidney Hertzberg, who was our fish meal broker when I had that business, came to me. "Lawrence," he said, "I have a group of friends in Rialto who want me to build them a golf course. I know of a piece of property that we can buy. If you want to go in with me, we can build that course. The people are going to organize. They will pay so much down. We'll have a good investment."

Richard, my boy, and I went to look at the property. We

agreed to go into the deal. We bought the land and started building the course during the time that the men were organizing the club. That procedure turned out to be a mistake. We should have let them organize and pay the money down, then build the course. Although we had started building, they didn't have enough members to make a down payment. They couldn't take over the club.

This meant that Mr. Hertzberg and I operated the course. He lived closer, in Ontario; so he supervised the course. We hired a regular manager, and we obtained a good pro, or professional golf instructor. Dutra was his name.

We ran the course for a couple of years, but it wasn't doing well. I went to Sidney one day and said, "I know that you'd like to own this golf course. You will never have a better chance than right now. Give me my money back. You pay all the bills and take the course. I'll give you three months to raise the money."

"O.K.," he replied.

Mary and I went to Europe. We were gone four and one-half months. (This was not our first trip there, by the way. My first trip back to my homeland was in 1948.)

When I came home, I went to see Mr. Hertzberg. He was in financial difficulty. He couldn't raise the money. "All right," I told him, "I'll give you the same terms in reverse. I'll give you back all the money that you put in. I'll pay the bills and I'll take the course."

He agreed.

We—our family—had formed ourselves into a corporation by then. Now we had a golf course and a pro shop, but we had no clubhouse. I talked to the members of my family—the rest of the corporation—and told them that we should build a clubhouse and make it a semi-membership. Someone could play whether he was a member or not. They agreed. We built a clubhouse and locker rooms, swimming pool, tennis courts, a new pro shop, snack bar, restaurant and cocktail bar. Our corporation has been operating the course ever since, with first Norman and now Doris managing. This is how we acquired El Rancho Verde Country Club.

By the time I had bought the golf course, I had formed the American Processing Corporation, to handle our diversified interests. In 1941, my old partner, Charles Landers, another man named Harold Hadley, and I bought a building which was situated on the southwest corner of Seventh Avenue and C Streets in San Diego. We operated the building for several year. Mr. Landers and Mr. Hadley now are deceased, but were well known in San Diego for many years.

In 1947, I decided to take my children into the business; so I gave each of them 15 percent. Mrs. Oliver and I retained 55 percent. We formed the American Processing Corporation, and issued stock accordingly. Later on, the corporation bought Mr. Hadley's interest in the building and eventually bought out Mr. Lander's interest, making the Oliver family the sole owner. Several years afterward, we bought the building next to it on Seventh Avenue. We continued to operate under this name until I sold out my meal business, in 1962.

Chapter XIX

A Return To The Azores—And A Little Trip To Europe

After World War II was ended, and conditions more or less had returned to normal, I was seized with an impulse. One day I said to Mary, "You know, Mary, I've been here in America for forty-five years, and I'd like to go back to my native land. I'd like to see the place where I was born."

Mary had never traveled to Europe. All that I was thinking of was revisiting my homeland, but she had other ideas. As women do, she pursued her objective in a round-about fashion.

"Why don't you go by yourself and see your country and then come back?" she suggested.

"No, Mary, I won't go unless you go."

"I'll tell you what—I'll go, but why don't we take a little trip to Europe, too?"

I agreed. The way it wound up, we took my sister and Doris, our daughter. Norman joined us in June. Richard was unable to go. The four of us, my wife and my sister and my daughter and I, left New York on March 27, 1948. It was my birthday and forty-five years to the day since the afternoon that I had leaped into the launch at São Miguel and had been taken aboard the steamer which brought me to the United States.

We were gone seven and one-half months, during which time we had many interesting experiences. Not all were pleasant, but all were interesting. The highlight of our trip was our audience with Pope Pius XII.

We stayed on the island of Pico, where I was born, for three months. During that time we made short trips to the islands of Faial, São Jorge, Graciosa, Terceira, São Miguel, Santa Maria and Madeira. We sold our old family home while we were there, also.

Without seeing them, you can't imagine the beauty of these islands. They are a wonderful place in which to spend a vacation. The one thing they lack is accommodations for tourists. When people who are from there return for a visit, they must move in with friends or relatives. This is what we did.

The island of São Miguel is the only one having fairly good hotels. Transportation between the islands is poor. Four small steamers make the round trip from Lisboa once each month. In the summer, little boats travel between the islands with cargo. They sometimes take passengers. This is unsatisfactory for most people, for there are no accommodations. In addition, the boats are so tiny that they bob about like corks, making a rough trip.

The island of Pico exports small quantities of cattle, wine, cheese, butter, whale oil, and fruits in season. Because of the steepness of the terrain, crops are raised in terraces, designed to prevent the soil from washing down the hillside and to facilitate tilling. Every two or three years, it is necessary to excavate, to bring the soil to the upper area of the terrace. This is most often done by hand. The soil is carried to the top in baskets borne on the shoulder.

A cobblestone road encircles the island. To reach private property, however, roads must be built by the property owner. Many of these places are too steep to reach, even by ox cart. This makes it necessary for the transporting of crops, supplies, and other items to be accomplished mostly by human exertion. Pastures for grazing the cows, which produce the milk for cheese, are carefully maintained, as they were when I was a boy. Oxen still are utilized to work the land wherever feasible. They also pull the two-wheel carts, as they did in my time. The people still work them about two years and then fatten them for export.

On some of the islands very little beef is used. Some people serve meat once a week, others only once in two weeks. Every family raises one or two hogs each year. When the hogs are slaughtered, the people save all the lard. The meat is salted. It must last throughout the year. Around the first of January, when the people butcher their hogs, they have a celebration, as they did when I lived there. In the same manner, when it is time to harvest grapes, they still get together to work and to have a good time.

In Pico, we stayed with a family of six. We had no bathroom. We took baths out of a washbowl. One person would stand guard outside the door while the other was inside, bathing. There, also, was an outhouse. Only a few places in the islands have running water. Mary remarked that it had been a long time since she had used an outhouse.

We enjoyed visiting with some of my old friends, mostly people of my age that I remembered. By and large, conditions on the island remained the same as when I had left, forty-five years before. There was one new house and a highway that the government had built. It went about three-quarters of the way around the island. The other one-quarter was a trail, the same as when I had left. Small gasoline generators provided the only electricity. Telephones were scarce—about one for each village. It was as though time had stood still there, but, for me, so much had happened. I had come back from another world.

My wife marveled, "I never knew night could be so black! There was almost no electric lighting. At night, it was dark as pitch. We could see all the stars. From a boat, when we passed the little villages, here and there would be a twinkle of light from an oil lamp shining out through the windows of the homes."

We wanted to see the Feast of Santo Cristo, which is held on the island of São Miguel, so we decided to go there for the ceremony. We planned to return to Pico in time to observe the Feast of the Pentecost, or Holy Spirit, which I especially wanted to celebrate in my home town.

The way things turned out, we darned near never saw anything. We were almost pitched in the sea and drowned. We took a little boat called the *Terralta*. It was her maiden voyage and almost her last. The engines kept breaking down. The trip, which should have taken twelve hours, took forty-eight. There was nothing to eat or drink on board, no accommodations whatsoever. She was a diesel, about eighty-five feet long, with twin screws, but, Lord, how she rode—like a bucking bronco at a rodeo.

Mary was scared. She kept praying, "Oh, dear Lord, we left America to have all of us die in the mid-Atlantic Ocean." She was sure we'd never step on land again.

The boat paused at every island. At first it picked up people. Finally, when conditions grew very bad on board, the captain started putting passengers off at the different islands, in order to wait for other boats. We kept hoping that he'd put us off. Why he left us, I don't know. It was no honor. It was our regret.

After we arrived at São Miguel and had a meal and a night's sleep, we felt much better, though. The people treated us royally. The ceremony was beautiful. My wife has studied the background of the statue and of the ceremony, and this is what she says: "A group of women on the island of São Miguel desired to start an order of nuns. They went to Rome to see the pope. He was so impressed with their ideas that he gave them permission and, also, gave them the statue of Santo Cristo, a torso. He has performed many miracles, they claim. There is a feast held in his honor every year. He is kept in the convent and is not exposed, except during one week just before Pentecost.

"The nuns tell many stories about the place and the statue. They showed us rose bushes which were two hundred years old, which were blooming in their garden. They told us one story of some burglars who plotted to get into the convent and at the statue. (It is adorned with many precious jewels that people have given—diamonds and rubies, and other priceless stones. We saw them ourselves when we visited in the island.) The burglars tried to climb a pear tree outside the wall, in order to get into the garden and into the convent, but when they started to climb the tree, their hands stuck to the limbs. The next morning the nuns found them, trapped.

"On the day of the ceremony the people take the statue out on the street and have a big procession. The men dress in tails. The highest officials of the islands carry the statue in something resembling a sedan chair. In his hands, the figure holds a sheaf, a replica of a corn stalk, made of gold. The tassels at the top of the corn stalk are pearls. The eyes of the statue are so real, you would swear he was ready to talk to you. He wears a beautiful cape, adorned with jewels, and has many different capes for the different seasons of the year. When we were at the convent, we saw all those capes and the jewels that go with them.

"We viewed the parade from an office. The statue is taken through the town and then around to the church. The church on the outside is decorated with little lights that design the walls. There is a bandstand in the plaza, decorated with the same tiny lights. The women dress in black, with black mantillas on their heads. Each one carries a candle. At night, a band plays Portuguese music. It's a most impressive ceremony."

When the festivities were over, Mary said to me, "Please, I don't want to return to Pico on any little boat. Let's wait for the steamer."

I agreed, gladly. We had a two weeks wait, but we enjoyed those two weeks. A friend of ours, Joe Medina, had brought a Dodge car from America. Since he could not take it to Pico in a small boat, he left the car with us; so we could bring it on the steamer. We hired a chauffeur for the two weeks and had a great time. We were entertained by the governor, the owner of the newspaper and the president of the bank.

I missed the main part of the Feast of the Pentecost, which I especially had wanted to see. I have never been able to celebrate a Pentecost in Pico since I left.

On the day of the festa, in addition to the sweetbread and wine and sky rockets, a cart, with a pair of oxen decorated with paper flowers, is displayed. The rusquilha is in the shape of a doughnut, only much bigger.

The people make their own firecrackers with a big chicken feather in which they put the powder. It becomes a quill fuse which they light and swoosh!

The inhabitants, also, do this when the Americans arrive. Once we got to the island at nine o'clock at night. One or two people showed up, then a priest arrived. Soon the bells of the church started to ring. Sky rockets burst in the air. I asked if someone had died. The priest said, "No, this is in your honor."

We had two other unusual experiences while in the islands and in Portugal. The first one occurred while we were on our way to Portugal from the Azores. Once again, I want my wife to describe the event: "We were headed for São Miguel, on our way to Portugal, and were out on the open sea, walking the deck when we heard a chorus of voices. It sounded almost as though the music came from Heaven. We didn't realize that we were right outside the island of Graciosa. The ship stopped. We walked around to the other side where we saw people bringing the statue of Our Lady of Fatima out to our boat. The statue was on a launch and was decorated with flowers at the base of her feet. The bishop, the nuns, and the priests were on that same boat. The people on the land and others following in little whale-boats, all tied to each other, were waving and singing goodby to her. 'Ave, ave, ave Maria,' they sang, and waved their hand-kerchiefs.

"As the launch approached our boat, all the higher officers went down to the bottom of the ladder and brought the statue on board. They placed her in a room fixed for her. She traveled with us during the rest of the voyage, which I imagine, was about three days. At the island of Terceira, the ship stayed for a day and a night. Pilgrims came on board, to visit her, to make promises, and to ask for favors, to pray and to sing.

"When we arrived at São Miguel, all the city officials and navy officials and children's groups came up the gangplank with

174

red roses. The officials took her on their shoulders and carried her in a procession into the little town of Ponta Delgada.

"The town has a plaza and a bandstand. There is a church on one side and a convent on the other. An outdoor altar with wreaths of flowers had been prepared. Flower petals were scattered on the ground at the foot of the statue. A mass was said. The sick and the crippled were blessed. The statue is taken from one island to another in this same manner."

They skipped Pico, though, my home island. The people were unhappy. The pastor from the parish where I was born gave me a letter to the bishop. I didn't get to see him, but I talked to his secretary and told him how the people from Pico felt. He said he would speak to the bishop.

Months later, the statue went to Pico. I don't know whether I had anything to do with it or not, but the people told me that they had a beautiful ceremony.

Our Lady of Fatima is very important to the Portuguese. It was at Fatima, a little village in central Portugal, on May 13, 1917, that a vision of a lady appeared to three young peasant children. They saw her each month until October 13. At that time, she identified herself as Our Lady of the Rosary and told the children that she wanted a chapel to be built on that spot. It was to be dedicated to the Virgin Mary. After that, she disappeared.

The story was verified and accepted by the bishop of the area. The first pilgrimage was held in 1927. Between May and October, on the twelfth and the thirteenth of each month, a ceremony is conducted at Fatima. People come to pray for world peace and for the sick, and so on. For this book my wife described the scene: "The people gather at night, when it grows dark. Each one carries his own candle. They take Our Lady of Fatima in a procession up to the plaza, about two blocks away. Thousands of people come. It's a magnificent sight, the dark, with a tremendous number of little candles lit and moving, moving, moving, as the people surge back and forth. They march until they become a solid mass of people and candles.

"The next day there is a mass and a procession. Bishops from different parts of the world come to participate in the mass. They bless the sick and the handicapped. People arrive from all over Portugal; by the bus loads; some on foot; some barefoot. They sleep on the ground.

"We stayed ten or twelve miles away and came for the night procession, then went home and came back again the next morning. We've been there every time that we've gone to Portugal."

We had made arrangements to see as much of Europe as we could, beginning with Portugal, then Spain, Italy, France, Switzerland, Holland, Germany, Austria, England, Scotland, Ireland, and Belgium. Mary attended the ceremony at Coimbra, also. We were intrigued with the different countries, their customs and their modes of living, which in most cases differed considerably from ours. My sister had returned home, to the states, but Mary and I and the children enjoyed the tour. I confess that I am not much of a traveler, though. Every time I turned around, I had to produce a ticket or a passport, or some document. My pockets bulged.

The event we most looked forward to was the audience with the pope. In order to be granted this audience, we had made the necessary arrangements with the bishop of San Diego, His Excellency, the Most Reverend Charles F. Buddy.

Bishop Buddy was San Diego's first bishop. He was consecrated on December 21, 1936, after the diocese of San Diego was formed from the Los Angeles diocese by the separation of the four southernmost counties of California. They are Riverside, Imperial, San Diego and San Bernardino. He entered the priesthood on September 19, 1914 and passed away on March 6, 1966. When he came here, we had sixty-three parishes and thirty-six grade schools. When he passed away, we had one hundred sixty-five parishes and eighty-seven elementary schools. The University of San Diego was his dream. He was a tremendous go-getter and, to him, nothing was more important than schools.

As I said, we spoke to him before we left San Diego. He gave us a letter of recommendation. When we arrived in Rome, we took it to the clerk at the hotel. The hotel took care of all reservations for us. This was in the summertime. We expected to be part of a general audience, but thanks to Bishop Buddy, who must have put in some kind words for us, we were given a private audience.

We first were ushered into a large reception room. Other people kept entering for the audience with Pope Pius XII. There were monks in different habits and nuns in costumes we had never seen before. Some were from India, some from Africa, from Asia—they were from everywhere.

While we sat, we heard our names called for a private audience with the pope. This was a surprise and a great honor. We were taken into a room filled with little alcoves, each big enough for two people. There was a distance of four or five feet between the alcoves and five or six alcoves in all.

When the pope came in, he began at the first alcove. We were in the last one. When he reached us, he said, "Oh, you are the Olivers from America. I have been in America. In fact, I was at the ecumenical council in San Francisco. I think that is a very beautiful city."

I told him, "I am American, but by naturalization. In reality, I am a Portuguese."

The pope replied, *Nos então vamos falar em português.* (We are going to speak in Portuguese.) He spoke in Portuguese all the time that we were with him.

Our son and daughter had not been invited to the private audience. They met him with the group. He talked to all these different people in their native tongues. When he came to Doris and Norman, he said, "Oh, I spoke to your mother and father on the inside."

We were very impressed by him. His knowledge of America

was astounding. It seemed that there wasn't a language which he couldn't speak. He knew something of the country of each of the people at the audience. He was a congenial type of person, very friendly, very much at ease with people.

One of the other places which we felt we had to see on this trip was the shrine of Lourdes, in France. We almost didn't make it, due to one of those episodes which always seem to occur when traveling in Europe and which make me not too fond of traveling.

Lourdes, of course, is world famous. This is where the Blessed Virgin appeared to a young girl named Bernadette Soubirous—later Saint Bernadette—eighteen times between February 11 and July 16, 1858. She showed the girl where there was a spring, with healing waters. She told her to have a chapel built there and to have the sick come to regain their health.

The first mass at Lourdes was held in 1871. Thousands of people come there every year. We got as far as a depot in Toulouse, where we were to take the train to Lourdes. There we had trouble. Our children, Doris and Norman, were the only ones who understood a little French. Neither Mary nor I knew a word. We saw a train. My wife said, "You kids ask if it is going to Lourdes." "Oh, yes, yes," the trainmen said in French; so we got on. (We noticed that we were the only passengers, but we didn't give it much thought — it was early.)

We selected a car, put our bags in it, and sat down. The lights were dim. Norman had talked us into buying him a guitar when we were in Lisboa. He took only about eight lessons on the thing, but he played the violin already, and music is easy for him. While we were waiting for some action, he pulled out his guitar and he started to strum away. As he played, we sat. We sat, and we sat, and we waited, and we waited. Still everything was dark. There were no lights on the train. We saw no other passengers. Mary told the kids, "Go out there and ask the brakeman if we are on the right train."

They went out and asked, "Train to Lourdes?"

"Yes, yes," the brakeman said, "train to Lourdes."

We sat some more. As Norman played, the rest of us stared at our watches. It was only a few minutes until train time, and still no action. "Go out there," Mary told the kids, "and ask them what time the train leaves."

This time the brakeman asked them what train they wanted. They said we were to take the "such-and-such a train."

"Oh," he said, "down there. There it is." He pointed to another train that was steaming away, about to go. The kids ran back to us and told us what was wrong. We flung open the windows of the car and threw our bags out. It's a wonder we didn't kill somebody passing by. We jumped off the train, grabbed the bags and ran across the tracks to the other train. It was about two blocks away. As we boarded the train, it started to move. The boy who took care of our room said, "I was wondering where you people were. Everything's here, waiting for you. What happened?"

The other train, we learned, was going to Lourdes, but didn't leave until the next morning.

Norman kept asking, "How come you're not singing, Dad?" while we were waiting in the wrong train.

I said, "I don't feel like singing."

At Lourdes, the people come every day for mass, and the sick go through the baths. Mary still talks of one incident that we saw: "It was a young man in a wheel chair pushed by his father. The boy's legs were pinched and thin. His arms were distorted, his face a blank. The moisture from the waters dripped from his ears.

"I never before saw a look resembling the expression on the father's face. His faith, was a light, shining through his face and eyes. He didn't look at any of us. He didn't see any of us. He pushed the cart with his grown son—such a cripple—and with that face filled with hope and faith that his son would be all right. I couldn't take my eyes off that father. We saw many sights like this, but I still can visualize him."

Although our trip was interesting and exciting, we were glad to return home to America. To be frank, I expected that trip to the Azores to be my swan song, never to go again, but I have returned several times. Each time I go, I am glad to see the places, but each time I realize how fortunate I was to have been able to come to the United States to live.

Chapter XX

Rewards For Good Deeds

In the 1950's I received three of my most prized awards. I was honored by both the Portuguese and Brazilian governments and was given the title of Knight of Saint Gregory, by the pope. This honor, being made a prince of the church, was, to me, the climax of my career. I could never ask for anything more than that; yet I do not mean to imply that I am not grateful for the other honors given me. I am—and I treasure them.

In December, during one year in the 1950's, the Portuguese Minister of Foreign Affairs, Dr. Paul Cunha, made a trip to Washington and then came through California. He arrived with a delegation. We held a banquet for him in the El Cortez Hotel, here. After the dinner, he presented decorations to three of us Portuguese-Americans. They were Manuel G. Rosa, M. O. Medina, and myself. Each of us received a medal and the title *Comandadore,* which means commandant, or captain, or officer.

We all had been active in the community. Mr. Rosa was important in the fishing industry. He had a policy of trying to name all of his boats with Portuguese names. I was responsible for some of those Portuguese names on the boats also, although I worked ashore. In addition, I had spent a good deal of time on Portuguese affairs. Mr. Medina had contributed much to the community, also. The award is given for the things that you do and, also, for the things that you achieve as a Portuguese-American. The Portuguese government keeps a check on what its people in other countries do.

With the Brazilians, the situation was a little different. Brazil has always been close to Portugal. It was discovered by a Portuguese explorer, Pedro Alvarez Cabal, in 1500. It was, for some time, a Portuguese colony. During the Napoleonic Wars, the Portuguese court was transferred from Lisboa to Rio de Janeiro. Later, the king, John VI, left his son, Pedro I, as emperor of Brazil. It has been an independent country since then, but it still is much like Portugal.

Since we spoke the same language, and our customs were so much alike, we Portuguese often were called upon to be of help with the Brazilians, when they came to San Diego. We entertained several of their high standing officials. For example, we entertained their Minister of War and their Ambassador from Washington, D.C. They were here one year for the *California Story,* which was part of the the *Fiesta del Pacifico,* a week dedicated to California history. It was held annually for a while, beginning in 1955. One year, it was dedicated to the governors of the United States. Another year, it was dedicated to the South American countries.

My wife and I once sang in the program, when it was held in the stadium behind San Diego High School. We wore fancy outfits, which she says were "squaw dresses and Spanish costumes."

At the time that the program was dedicated to the South American countries, the city invited the representatives of the Brazilian government to come here. The city asked us to play host to them, which we were glad to do.

Later, after everything was over, one day I was called up to the El Cortez Hotel. There the Brazilian government presented me with the medal and the title of *Comandadore.* Another person who received the same award was John Athaide, who for many years has been a vice-president of the U.S. National Bank. He is of Portuguese descent, although he was born in Massachusetts, and is the same person who recommended U.S. National Bank to me when it opened.

The Minister of War gave Mary a large aquamarine stone which she had made into a ring. It is five or six carats—a very nice piece of jewelry. We were impressed with the generosity of the Brazilian representatives.

As I said, though, I consider my highest honor, the greatest of honors that I could be given, was my Knight of Saint Gregory title. This is the highest honor that can be bestowed on a layman by the Catholic Church.

The Order of Saint Gregory was founded by Gregory the Great, in 1831, and reformed by Pope Pius X, in 1905. Qualifications include an unblemished character and a history of promoting the interests of both society in general and the Catholic Church.

The Church works through the parishes and the diocese to get the names of people recommended for the title. I was notified by our parish priest, Monsignor Lawrence Forrestal, that I was going to receive this honor. (Monsignor Forrestal served at Saint Agnes Church from 1935 until 1963. He passed on in September of that year.) I was requested to get my measurements from a tailor and send them to Italy to have my uniform made. The costume is striking, including a plume hat and a sword.

This is the mass during which I was made a Knight of Saint Gregory.

Sunday, August 22, 1954, Bishop Buddy came to Saint Agnes Church, my parish church, and bestowed the honor on me. There is a mass, much like a regular mass. At the end you have become a prince of the church.

When the bishop needs us for some ceremony, the Knights of Saint Gregory form a procession before him. At the time that I received my award, Monsignor Forrestal said that it was for good works and good deeds, many of which had never been made public.

My Knight of Saint Gregory uniform. It is green, with gold trim, a very beautiful costume.

Chapter XXI

The Early Sixties

In 1962, I celebrated my seventy-fifth birthday with a surprise party given by my wife. I also sold the American Processing Company, a business which I had owned for forty years.

If you remember, I changed the name of my firm from American Fisheries to American Processing Company in 1947, when I formed a corporation including my wife and my children. We functioned under this name until June, 1962. Earlier that year a Mr. Peterson, of the Peterson Manufacturing Company of Los Angeles, came to San Diego to ask if we would like to sell the business. We told him that if the firm really was interested, we would be glad to talk about it. He assured us that he was in earnest. I wanted him to inspect the plant before we started our talks. This he did.

Upon his return, he remarked, "You have quite a place here. What do you want for it?"

I told him that I would quote him a price subject to the possibility of transferring the leases which we had with the city of San Diego and the Santa Fe Railway. After he received the price, he went to Los Angeles to talk to his board of directors. He was to let me know the decision within two weeks.

In two weeks he was back to inform me that, "We will buy the plant at your price."

He made a deposit. I started the papers. The deal was completed on June 22, 1962, which, you might remember, was exactly forty years from the day that I had signed up to move into that building. When I signed the contract of sale, I could not help thinking of the difference in my circumstances from that earlier day. Bigger dreams than I had ever dreamed had come true. I knew that it was because I worked hard, had the help of God, the encouragement of my family and assistance from some wonderful friends.

We still had some business left; however, the name of the American Processing Company went with the business which we sold. This meant that we had to form another corporation to handle the fishing boats, the buildings at Seventh and C Streets, and El Rancho Verde Country Club. The new corporation was called the Circle L Investment Corporation.

Before this event occurred, however, on March 27, my seventy-fifth birthday, my wife gave me a surprise party. Months in advance she started to plan. My wife is happiest when she is planning something for someone. She wrote letters to all of our relatives, from San Diego clear up into Oregon. She rented a box in the post office, so that the answers would go there. Later she nearly had a fit because the post office misunderstood her request and held back all the mail. She said, "I thought, 'Ye Gods and little fishes, Lawrence will be wondering what happened to the mail'; so I ran down to the post office to straighten things out."

I never was one bit suspicious. She made arrangements for the party to be held at the U.S. Grant Hotel, two days before my birthday. She told me that we had an invitation to a party on that date for two very good friends. I agreed to go, never suspecting anything. The night of the party, however, she spent so much time getting dressed that I thought we would never get there. I couldn't understand this. Mary usually is prompt. Finally she was ready; so we left. I imagined we'd be the last ones to arrive and, sure enough, we were. I didn't know that this was pre-arranged.

We reached the hotel and went to the room. Everything seemed so quiet that I asked her if she had the right date. She assured me that she was correct. It seemed odd, though. There was no sound, no action, even the room was dark. As we reached the door everyone yelled, "Surprise!" and the lights came on.

The first person I saw was our older son—and his family—and then all our relatives and friends. There were 135 people there, even an orchestra.

Mary was unprepared for the large response. She had counted on only a few people accepting, but almost everyone responded.

She set up a main table for our family. Down the center of the room were our godchildren and their families. On the right side was my family and on the left side was her family. Employees who had worked with me for thirty years or more, and friends whom we had known for forty years, were there. Mary had a photograph of me taken—this was some time earlier. Everyone received a copy. I autographed them all.

The party was a great success. Mary was happy because she had done something to make me happy. She never forgets—except where it concerns herself, as she did that night, she later confessed: "I did forget something. I forgot to find myself a place to sleep. We had many guests from out of town for the night. I figured this bed for this person, this room for that person, so many pillows and sheets and blankets. I had everybody settled, including Lawrence—whom I put in the maid's room (without the maid, he always adds)—and I turned around, and I had no place to sleep, no blankets, no pillows, no bed. I slept on the couch in the living room, wearing two bathrobes and bed socks."

One of the things with which I always have been blessed is good health. Aside from being somewhat frail when I was born and the severe attack of typhoid fever when I was a young man, I hardly ever knew what it was to be ill.

Towards the end of 1964, however, I began to experience some physical discomfort. I had severe pains in my left arm. The first time that I really noticed this was on a day when Mary and I were riding to San Marcos, up near Escondido, about forty miles from here. We had my wife's brother, Horace Miller, with us, and his wife, who is called Susie. We were going for dinner there. On the way, I had to stop the car. I explained to them that I had a terrible, oh, it was a terrible pain in my arm. I walked around a bit, and it eased off.

Later, I talked to my doctor, who told me that I was experiencing some heart trouble. This presented a problem, for my wife and I had already made a commitment to be in Lisboa, Portugal, between December 8 and December 16. We had been invited to be delegates to the first congress of Portuguese communities throughout the world. It was headed by the Geographic Society of Lisboa, whose president, Adriano Moreira, had traveled to Portuguese communities all over the world to invite the people to come to the *Congresso*. We wanted to attend. My doctor gave his permission; so we went.

At the *Congresso,* various committees which were composed of the representatives from the Portuguese settlements, dealt with specific problems, such as improving communications between Portuguese communities, preserving the culture of Portugal, and so on.

There were no expenses paid, with the exception of the hotel expense while we were there. We were amazed at the number of people who attended from over the world—Brazil and Japan —Africa, almost every place that you could think of. All the groups had an opportunity to speak. Mary spoke and in Portuguese, too. Her speech was on the establishment of the Society of Queen Santa Isabel. She was the official representative of the society. She explained how it was organized and for what purpose and the achievements of the group.

She began by saying, *Luzo Americano*—"I am an American." That was to let the audience know that Portuguese was not her native language. She spoke it, as she says, "as I heard it spoken in my home as a child."

Her speech went over well. I guess they admired her nerve. People hugged her and embraced her afterward. There were about 400 people in attendance. I was proud of her.

One other couple went from San Diego, Tony Cudinha and his wife. Mr. Cudinha is very active in the Cabrillo Day celebration, when Cabrilho's landing here is re-enacted each year.

I was made a director. The *Congresso* is held every other year, that's one of the things which was decided at that first meeting. Because of my health, I since have tendered my resignation, but apparently they haven't accepted it. They still send me the literature and the invitations.

We were taken to visit many interesting places and were given a reception. The way the Portuguese treated us was wonderful. One of the most interesting features was hearing the delegates from Malaca talk. They speak sixteenth century Portuguese, which no one else does.

Most people don't even know where Malaca is. The term is an old name for the Malay Peninsula, which the Portuguese conquered, in 1511. For a long time afterward they controlled the trade in spices and tin, until they lost the area to the Dutch, in 1641. The Portuguese spoken in Malaca dates from the original conquest. Malaca now is a state of Malaya, in the federation of Malaysia. There, also, is a town of the same name.

The *Congresso* inauguration ceremonies were held in the auditorium of the Geographic Society. The President of the Republic of Portugal, Admiral Americo Thomaz, was there. Manuel Cardinal de Cerejeira, Patriarch of Lisboa, attended. Experts in all fields of Portuguese life, economic, military, social, and political were participants.

The *Congresso* adopted resolutions establishing the Union of Portuguese Communities of Culture; forming an organization called the *Academia International da Cultura Portuguesa,* or the International Academy of Portuguese Culture; creating a fund to support fellowships for post-graduate work in Portuguese cultural studies, both in Portuguese territory and in other countries; and deciding that future meetings be held alternately in Portugal and in other lands.

It was an impressive affair. We were glad that we had the opportunity to attend. Mary and I regret that we have not been able to go to any of the sessions since then.

189

For my wife, though, in one way, I know that it was a worrisome journey, for she was concerned about my health. I did experience some chest pain on the way over and, as the plane landed, I also had the severe arm pain come back. Mary tells me now that all the time she was there at the convention she was silently praying, "Oh, dear God in Heaven, get us back to America safe and sound."

She gave no surface indication of her worries, though, and her prayers were answered. We arrived back in the States around the middle of December, in time to have a wonderful Christmas with our family and our friends. We always have enjoyed the holidays.

On the sixth of January, I suffered a bad heart attack. Mary and I were having dinner when I began feeling the distress in my arm and chest. I told my wife, "I can't eat. I have such a terrible pain."

She knows me well enough after all these years to realize that when I can't eat, I must be pretty sick. I have never had trouble with eating or sleeping.

The doctor came. He gave me a shot and told her to watch me. She prayed and watched, and when I grew worse, she called the doctor back. They rushed me to the hospital. Within half an hour of my arrival, I experienced a massive heart attack. I thought "This is it. I'm going." Nobody ever wants to go, I guess, not many anyway, but I've had a wonderful life. I had no complaints. I said a little prayer, "Dear Lord, whatever you decide for me, I'm ready."

I guess He wasn't ready for me. I was in the hospital for five and one-half weeks, though. Since that time I have enjoyed some wonderful experiences, including our fiftieth wedding anniversary, which we celebrated with our entire family later that same year.

An odd situation came up after I had my heart attack. I remembered that I had a first communion in the old country, but I could never remember being confirmed. After I had my heart attack, in 1965, the bishop that we had then, Bishop Furey, came to see me. I told him I did not know whether I had ever been confirmed. The bishops in the islands only visited every few years. I asked him what you would do in a case like that. Here I was, going on eighty years of age, and having received all sorts of awards, and never been confirmed.

He said, "Don't worry. I'll take care of that. You and your family come to my house. I will say mass for you and I will confirm you in the chapel."

That's what he did. My youngest son, Norman, stood up for me while I was being confirmed. Monsignor Joseph Trivisonno, the well-known Italian priest from Our Lady of the Rosary Church, was there (he's passed away since, in February 1969); so was Monsignor John Purcell and a few others. We gave a dinner that night. I told the guests that I felt as though I were starting life over again.

They kidded me about having Norman stand up for me. "Why not?" I asked. "I stood up for him many a time."

Chapter XXII

A Golden Wedding Anniversary

The year 1965, in addition to being the year in which I had my heart attack, was also our fiftieth wedding anniversary. My wife and I discussed at great length how we should celebrate this occasion, especially in view of the fact that I nearly didn't live to see it. We felt that we wanted to do something that would be meaningful for our children and grandchildren, as well as for us. What should we do, we asked ourselves.

We still were undecided when one day our son, Norman, accidentally hit the nail on the head. He, our daughter, Doris, and my wife and I were discussing the matter when Norman spoke up, half-way kidding, and said, "Why don't you take all of us to Portugal to celebrate your anniversary?"

We laughed. I said, "Young man, I took you to Europe once. If you go again, you go at your own expense."

We dropped the subject, but Norman had planted the seed, as the saying goes. Somehow we kept coming back to that idea. Gradually it grew into the concept of taking the children and grandchildren on a trip to Europe and having an audience with the pope, if we could, in honor of the occasion.

We did feel disturbed about the money. As Mary said, "It will cost a lot of money. Maybe it isn't right to spend so much money this way. When we pass on, we will leave the children that much less, and maybe they will need the money sometime."

We'd talk some more. We felt, as she put it, "that it would be the experience of a lifetime for us and, more important, for the children and the grandchildren. They would have wonderful memories of us all together on that trip, and memories are worth a great deal. We decided to do it—and we've been glad ever since that we did."

Once we made up our minds we thought that we might as well shoot for the moon. We wanted the whole family to participate in an audience with Pope Paul VI. (Paul VI became pope in June 1963, after Pope John XXIII passed away. We never had the privilege of meeting Pope John. We regret this, for he was a man of inspiration.) The audience, as my wife pointed out "would include youngsters down to four years of age."

Once again we went to the bishop for help. As I mentioned before, our bishop at that time was the Most Reverend Francis J. Furey, who came here on July 25, 1963, to assist Bishop Buddy. He succeeded Bishop Buddy on March 6, 1966. He left this area in 1969, after being appointed Archbishop of San Antonio, Texas.

We spoke to Bishop Furey, who said that he would be in Rome at that time, attending the second ecumenical council. He would see what he could do for us, as far as a family visit with the pope was concerned. He didn't bat an eye over the idea of taking all the children.

We started making plans. Soon Mary had another idea. One day while at our daughter's home in Rialto, she said, "You know, Doris, we met Pope Pius XII and received blessings and so many good things and here we go again, with the whole family. This is going to be a very special occasion. I would like to take him something."

"Mother," Doris asked, "what in the world could you take to the pope?"

Mary replied, "Well, I don't know, but I would like to take him something. Give me your missal."

Doris gave her the prayer book and Mary went through it, looking at all the pictures. She came across one that had the three-tiered pope's crown, with the two keys of heaven and a little papal seal underneath. "This is it. I'm going to take this to a jeweler to see if I can't have a pair of cuff links made with this inscription on them."

That's what she did. They were beautiful—I must admit that. She took them along on our trip. We didn't all fly together. Instead, we met at the airport in Rome. I suppose that my wife is the first woman in history to land in Rome carrying cuff links for the pope in her suitcase. When we arrived in the city, we called Bishop Furey. He came to see us that evening. "I think everything's going to work out fine," he said. "How is your transportation to Saint Peter's?"

"We have hired a twenty-passenger bus which we are going to use in every city that we visit."

"All right, you come to the Hotel Victoria and pick me up tomorrow, and we will go to Saint Peter's together."

Mary had the cuff links on her mind. "I don't know whether I'm doing the right thing or not." She told him about the gift.

The interior of Saint Peter's Cathedral, a most inspiring structure.

"Let me see them," he suggested. After he looked at the gift, he said, "You bring that package with you tomorrow."

That tomorrow and the rest of the trip, turned out to be "quite a day," as my wife said. I must use her words, since I sometimes was resting, rather than sightseeing with the rest of the family: "That morning our guide was curious. We weren't doing things the way she thought we should. She kept rushing up to us, asking, 'You got tickets to get in Saint Peter's?'

"We said, 'You stop at the Victoria Hotel and pick up the bishop. We'll take care of the rest.'

"She kept repeating, 'If you do not have tickets to get in, this is a waste of time.'

"We told her, 'Well, you take us to Saint Peter's. That's all you have to do—just get us there.'

"We stopped at the Victoria and picked up Bishop Furey and another bishop. He was from Washington. When we reached Saint Peter's, instead of stopping in front of the cathedral, we went around to the side. The guards opened the gates and our little bus went inside. There we got out. Bishop Furey cautioned, 'Now, you be sure to all hold hands. There are sixteen of us. Do not break away. Hang on to the children.'

"The youngest child, as we said, was only four, the next one was six, one eight, and then on up to sixteen years of age. We hung together for dear life. The bishop had the letter to get us in and had made all the arrangements. We approached a man dressed in tails and white tie. He read the letter and let us through. Next we went through the Swiss Guard. At last we all were inside. The pope's throne was directly in front of us. The bishops sat in the first row, before the throne. There was a row of about fifty or seventy-five bishops. This, as we said, was during the ecumenical council. Bishop Furey was seated on the second seat. We were directly behind him. He told us, 'As each bishop comes in, I'm moving down, because I want to be at the end by the time the pope comes in. When we begin to move, you come immediately behind me. Don't let anyone get beween us.'

"After we were seated, he said, 'Mary, let me see that box you've got for the pope.' He showed it to all the bishops. They admired it, but all the time I was thinking, 'What if he doesn't use cuff links!'

"It was 3:30 p.m. when we sat down. The pope did not appear until 5:00 that afternoon. During the hour and a half that we sat, I was on pins and needles. I thought, 'My Lord in Heaven, how will we keep nine children, the oldest sixteen, sitting still in a church for an hour and a half?' I had the most concern for Doris, for her three boys were all less than ten years old. She was sitting behind Bishop Furey. Soon there was a little commotion. He turned to her and whispered, 'Doris, what's going on back there?'

" 'My sons say they are thirsty.' He stuck his hand down in his pocket and brought out a little tin of hard candy. 'Pass these around. It will keep them busy for a while.'

"They were content for a little bit. Again, there was a little disturbance. 'Doris, what's going on now?'

" 'Oh, Bishop Furey, my little fellow (the four year old) says he has to go. What will I do?'

"The bishop turned around. He looked at Christopher. 'Christopher, you just forget it. You hear me? Just forget it!'

"Little Christopher stared at him like 'Do you mean it?' The bishop kept staring back; so Christopher let out a big sigh, laid his head in his mother's lap and went to sleep.

"When the pope finally appeared and raised his arms to give the blessing, I said to myself, 'Thank God, he's wearing cuff links!'

"After he finished speaking and congratulating all the other bishops, he reached Bishop Furey. The bishop introduced us and explained that this was the Oliver family from America. He told the pope that we were celebrating our fiftieth wedding anniversary, and that we had brought all our children and grandchildren for the celebration. This seemed to impress him. Lawrence handed him the gift. He appeared surprised and

The Oliver family being received by Pope Paul VI. In the foreground is Christopher, with his mother. Behind Doris is Richard's son, Rick. Bishop Furey is at the far right. Mary and I are in front, at the left. Richard is behind us.

The audience with Pope Paul VI, in 1965. Bishop Furey is number six from the left. Next to him are Doris, Joseph, Drew, and Christopher.

pleased. He was a much more introverted man than Pope Pius XII. His feelings did not show through nearly so much, but he must have a very tender place in his heart for children. The first person he touched was the little four-year-old. His face lit up when he looked at the boy. He put his hands in a gentle fashion on the tiny face while he blessed him. Then he touched the rest of us and blessed us in Latin. The next day he sent each of us a gold medal. Our guide couldn't get over the experience, 'I've never been so close to a pope in my life,' she said, 'and you didn't even have tickets.'

"The bishop gave us three evenings of his time, to show us around Rome, particularly the churches and the restaurants. As we'd walk down the street, he would always have Christopher by the hand. Christopher was tiny, and Bishop Furey is both large and tall, an imposing man. Everyone turned to look at the odd pair, strolling down the street together, talking and swinging hands.

"We thought that the children might grow tired of the traveling, but they behaved well. We took paper, crayons, picture books, chewing gum, balloons, and games; in order that they could entertain themselves in the bus. They enjoyed the sightseeing, and they enjoyed each other's companionship. The big ones took care of the little ones. They insisted on being seated together at meal time. I once made the mistake of dividing them up among the adults, but that idea didn't go over at all.

"Lawrence quite often stayed behind in the hotel while we went visiting. He was taking things easy because of his heart attack, but he did well while we were traveling. We had no problems.

"From Rome, we went to Madrid and on to Lisboa. We stayed about six days and had our anniversary dinner at the Ritz Hotel there. Lawrence always says that the dinner wasn't good, but the cake was beautiful. The hotel fixed us a lovely anniversary cake.

"We were so glad at the time and still are so glad that we

Our fiftieth wedding anniversary dinner, at the Ritz Hotel, in Lisboa. From the left are: Doris, Norman, Mary, Richard, his wife, De Von; grandchildren, Marie Christopher, Renée, Rick, Drew, Tom, Stephen, and Mark; Norman's wife, Lillian, and myself.

decided to make that trip. It put something special into all our lives. It brought us closer together as a family, and, I think, will always be a link between our grandchildren.

"Lawrence and I stayed two weeks after the rest of the family came home. When the grandchildren came to bid us goodby, I said, 'Oh, I know you must be very happy because you are going home.'

"They answered no, no, they weren't happy.

" 'Why? Why aren't you happy to go home?'

" 'Oh, we love to travel, so we'd rather stay here with you!'

"They still remember the trip. Five years later, when we had our fifty-fifth anniversary, we threw a party in the Palm Room of the U.S. Grant Hotel. Christopher came up to me with a long face. 'Vavó, why are you throwing a party for your anniversary?'

" 'Why, don't you think it's a nice thing to have a party?'

" 'No, we would have much rather gone to Europe.' "

Our fiftieth wedding anniversary cake.

Chapter XXIII

More Trips And Tributes

My wife and I have traveled quite a bit—abroad and elsewhere during the past twenty or more years. I could take the time because Richard was managing the plant; then when I sold it and retired, I had more spare time.

In the latter part of September, 1967, Mary and I decided to make another trip to the Azores. We flew to Lisboa. After resting and visiting for a few days, we went on to the islands by steamer. We wanted to see all of the islands of the Azores, with the exception of Flores and Corvo, once more, and probably for the last time.

The steamer stops at each of the islands to discharge cargo and passengers. This gave us plenty of time to rent a taxi, in order to circle the island and do a certain amount of sightseeing.

When we arrived at the island of Pico, there were at least a dozen friends waiting for us. We stayed there for ten days. The Reverend Adolfo Ferreira is pastor at the town of Bandeiras. He took us to his summer home in the *Cachorros,* a beautiful coastal place in which to spend a summer vacation. This resort area has an interesting history. Over 100 years ago a volcano erupted on the island of São Jorge and the hot lava poured across the island and into the sea. It traveled through the channel, to Pico. The width of the channel is about five miles, but from the volcano to Pico the distance is around fifteen miles. By the time the lava reached the point now known as the *Cachorros,* it had cooled enough to be molded into a series of unusual formations. One of the most striking of these is the head of a young dog. The word *cachorro* means young dog. The government has made a pavillion and a lookout at the site. It is something worth seeing. There, also, is a chapel called *Nossa Senhora dos Milagres,* Our Lady of Miracles, at Cachorros.

It was not just the scenery which made our visit pleasant. Father Ferreira and his family did all that they could for us. We had the use of their home, with meals, cooking and laundry done for us.

He took us all over the island in his car, anywhere that we wanted to go. If for some reason he couldn't go, his sister, Luzia, would take us. She is a professor in one of the schools, but was on vacation at the time. She was with us a great deal, a most pleasant companion.

Sometimes, if they both were busy, we would order a taxi. All we needed to do was to name the time, and the taxi would be there. In reality, the ten days we spent on this trip we enjoyed more than the three months we spent on our previous trip. We visited old friends in Villa das Lages, Santa Cruz das Ribeiras, Madalena, Cais do Pico, Piedade and such, but mostly in Calheta, because that is my home town.

I suppose that people may grow tired of hearing me say how lovely those islands are, yet I never cease being amazed at their beauty—no matter how often I visit them.

The people of the Azores are a very friendly people. They are delighted to do you a favor, and would do almost anything to make your visit enjoyable. In fact, the only thing which might irritate them would be if you wanted to do something, needed something, and didn't tell them. They like the Americans, and most of them wish that they had the opportunity to come to America. I realize how they feel, because at one time I wished the same thing. In my case it happened, and I will never stop thanking God for that blessing. There is a lot of criticism of this country, and I know that the United States is not perfect, but I have traveled over the better part of the world, and basically, this is the best country of all.

Left, to right; my *Comandadore* medal from Brazil, Mary's *Pro Pontifice et Ecclesiae* medal, and my *Knight of Saint Gregory* medal.

My *Comandadore* awards from the Portuguese government.

Here my wife, Mary, receives her *Pro Pontifice et Ecclesiae* award from the Most Reverend Leo T. Maher, who became bishop of San Diego on August 27, 1969. Previous to coming here, he was the first bishop of the Santa Rosa diocese, in northern California.

I am fond of this picture. It seems to me that it symbolizes everything which my wife stands for; love of country, devotion to her church, and the patient, unselfish characteristics of women.

Bishop Furey here confirms me. I was in my late seventies. My son, Norman, is behind me.

PRESENTED TO

LAWRENCE OLIVER

IN RECOGNITION AND APPRECIATION
OF 18 YEARS DEDICATED SERVICE
AS A DIRECTOR OF
SAN DIEGO
GAS & ELECTRIC COMPANY

FROM
THE DIRECTORS AND OFFICERS
APRIL 27, 1965

This closeup is of the plaque which I was given when I retired from the board of directors of the San Diego Gas and Electric Company, in 1965.

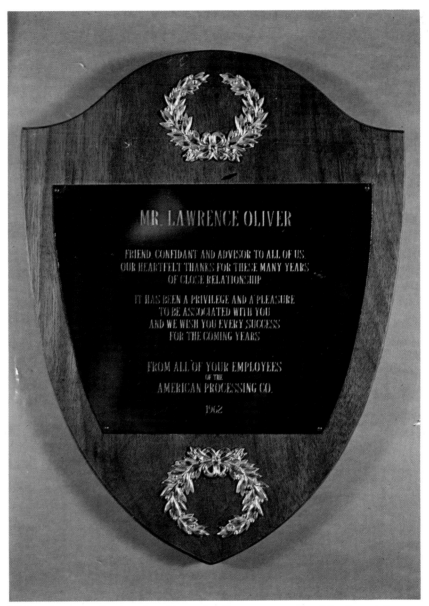

My employees at the American Processing Company gave me this plaque when we sold the business, in 1962. It reads, "Friend, confidant, and advisor to all of us. Our heartfelt thanks for the many years of close relationship. It has been a privilege and a pleasure to be associated with you and we wish you every success for the coming years." This tribute touched me. I always tried to be more than just a boss.

After we sold the American Processing Company, my family, the officers and the members of the board of directors presented me with this award. It reads that they are expressing to me "their appreciation for the fine leadership and outstanding devotion to the company for the past five decades."

When the League of Portuguese-American organizations held a testimonial dinner for me, in 1970, one of the gifts given to Mary and myself, was this electric clock, a present from the Portuguese-American Social and Civic Club.

The longer that we live, the more my wife and I seem to be blessed. It appears that there is no end to the kindness which has been extended to us by our fellow citizens. Mary has said, "Where will it end?" and "Whoever would dream that such wonderful things would happen to two little pip-squeaks like us?"

In 1968, the *San Diego Evening Tribune* interviewed many business, civic, and cultural leaders in a series of articles called "Building San Diego."

I was one of those interviewed. The article referred to me as a "civic leader, churchman, philanthropist, businessman, and innovator." I find it difficult to relate these remarks to me, but I am grateful for them.

In 1970, I was recognized by three organizations. The Women's Guild of Temple Emanu-El of San Diego honored me at its annual Gentlemen of Distinction dinner, held at the El Cortez Hotel in January. The dinner is a tribute to men who over the years have contributed to San Diego. They are selected from all walks of life. Over 600 people attended this dinner.

A short while later, the League of Portuguese-American organizations held a testimonial dinner for me at the U.S. Grant Hotel. A great number of my friends and business associates were invited. The league presented me with a picture of the statue of João Rodriques Cabrilho, and the Portuguese-American Social and Civic Club gave me an electric clock.

In April, the San Diego region of the National Conference of Christians and Jews held its forty-second anniversary citation dinner. It honored three San Diegans for their contributions toward promoting understanding among and between Christians and Jews. Burt Raynes, a founder of Rohr Corporation, Dr. A. P. Nasatir, of San Diego State College, and I were the three guests of honor.

Mr. Raynes was praised for his "important contributions to the cultural and commercial development of San Diego;" Dr. Nasatir for his "exceptional academic and humanitarian ser-

The Women's Guild of Temple Emanu-El
San Diego, California

honors

Lawrence Oliver

Gentleman of Distinction

for his years of service of lovingkindness
and the betterment of the San Diego Community
and of humanity
in the area of

Religion, Catholic

"It hath been told thee, O man, what is good,
And what the Lord doth require of thee;
Only to do justly, to love mercy,
And to walk humbly with thy God."
(Micah VI, 8)

January 24, 1970

My Gentleman of Distinction Award. It reads that I am being honored "for his years of service of lovingkindness and the betterment of the San Diego Community and of humanity in the area of Religion, Catholic.

"'It hath been told thee, O man, what is good,
"'And what the Lord doth require of thee;
"'Only to do justly, to love mercy,
"'And to walk humbly with thy God.'"

Micah VI, 8

vices;" and I for my "extraordinary service to church and community for more than half a century."

My wife, over the years, has given much of herself to our church and our community. In 1971, I was pleased to see her receive recognition for her hard work. On February 14, she was awarded the *Pro Pontifice et Ecclesiae* award, a papal decoration instituted by Pope Leo XIII for services to the church. For Pope and Church, the title translates.

Twenty people, men and women were recognized for their efforts in behalf of the Catholic Church. This was the largest single group ever to be awarded papal honors here.

206

The San Diego Region

The National Conference of Christians and Jews

CITES

Lawrence Oliver

For his extraordinary service to his church and his community for more than half a century. Recognized by his church with its highest lay award, the Knight of St. Gregory, presented by Pope Pius XII and honored by private audiences with Pope Pius XII and Paul VI. Mr. Oliver was also honored by his native Portugal and the Government of Brazil. San Diegans have Mr. Oliver to thank for its most famous landmark, the Cabrillo Statue and less privileged children of all races and religions in this area who have enjoyed Camp Oliver, are aware of his gift for the young to enjoy. An immigrant from Pico Island in the Azores, Oliver exemplifies the American dream of financial success which he has consistently shared with his fellow man in the spirit of Brotherhood.

Dudley W. Brown
President

Chairman

Co-Chairman

April 16, 1970
San Diego, California

My award from the National Conference of Christians and Jews: "For his extraordinary service to his church and his community for more than half a century. Recognized by his church with its highest lay award, the Knight of St. Gregory, presented by Pope Pius XII and honored by private audiences with Pope Pius XII and Paul VI. Mr. Oliver was also honored by his native Portugal and the Government of Brazil. San Diegans have Mr. Oliver to thank for its most famous landmark, the Cabrillo Statue and less privileged children of all races and religions in this area who have enjoyed Camp Oliver, are aware of his gift for the young to enjoy. An immigrant from Pico Island in the Azores, Oliver exemplifies the American dream of financial success which he has consistently shared with his Fellow man in the spirit of Brotherhood."

(During my lifetime I have been assisted by many people, who did not ask me what my religion was, or my nationality, or my political beliefs. I have tried to follow this same policy in my conduct toward others.)

The service was held at the Immaculata. The ceremony was impressive. The women wore black gowns with long sleeves and high necklines. They also wore black mantillas. I though that they appeared a little as though they were in mourning, but it was a memorable occasion and Mary looked very nice. She was overcome. "I never dreamed that I would ever receive such an award," she said. "I was thrilled and humbled. The bishop made the awards, and I received a beautiful medal."

207

He told her that her recognition was long overdue. Now she is Lady Mary and I'm Sir Lawrence.

A few days later, on February 28, 1972, my wife was given another honor. A group of ladies from a Portuguese organization that she belongs to gave her a testimonial luncheon. Once again she was surprised.

And, on May 7, 1972, she was honored, as I said, at the fiftieth anniversary celebration of the founding of Council Number 123, of the Society of Queen Saint Isabel.

Chapter XXIV

Portuguese Christmas and New Year Celebrations

M y wife enjoys telling a little story. She says it has a moral. "We had a strange thing happen after one of our trips to Europe. We were looking at some color slides we had taken. There was one that we couldn't identify. It was a beautiful view, out over a harbor, with hills and mountains behind a city. We wondered, 'Where in the world can this be?'

"Doris, my daughter, kept looking at the slide. 'Mother,' she said, 'that picture was taken here, right from this house. It's the bay and San Diego.'

"Sure enough, that's what it was. It was the prettiest picture we took, with the bay and the lights and the city. Wasn't that strange? We went so many thousand miles, and the most lovely scene we saw was right here at home.

"I guess that's the way our lives have been. Our happiest experiences have been in our home, with our friends and our family. We have had so many, many good times and have so many, many wonderful recollections. This house is full of happy, happy memories of parties and holidays, and other gatherings."

My Christmas at home in the Azores was altogether different from here, nothing but church celebrations, no gifts exchanged, nothing like that. Every community has a church. They have Little Christmas and the Three Kings. I think it is held on the sixth of January. People dressed up as the three kings go from door to door, singing carols which tell a story about the birth of Christ.

On New Year's Eve, they do the same thing. The singers go from door to door, and everyone gives them a drink. They have what we call an open house.

Here we spent many a New Year's Eve singing at the homes of our friends. We would go from door to door, sometimes to sixteen or more homes in one night, caroling.

We'd stand, singing, outside the front door. The hosts would open the door. We would finish our songs inside, those that could get inside. Along toward the end, the group of singers would be so big that no house could take them all.

In the houses the table was set, something to eat, something to drink. I always drank straight whiskey. "It's good for my voice," I would tell the host. "I'm singing tenor."

It would be cold, the middle of the night, maybe one or two o'clock in the morning. We'd get out under the street lights on the corners and sing and dance in the middle of the street.

People would come by in cars and would stop to listen. At midnight on New Year's, the bells would ring. Everyone would toot his car horn and shoot firecrackers. People would kiss each other and wish each other *Um Feliz Ano Novo,* a Happy New Year. The police would come by and stand, watching us. They never said anything. They enjoyed the festivities. You couldn't do that now. You'd get arrested; but we did it for many, many years, right here in Point Loma.

When you go singing at New Year's, you make up a verse appropriate to the family that you are visiting, something funny, and you sing it. Sometimes we sang in four voices, singing and answering each other.

"We'd come here last," Mary recalls. "The Christmas tree would be up, in the window overlooking the bay. I'd have a huge pot of coffee and food on the dining room table. We'd eat and drink and then go downstairs to the rumpus room. We'd push the pool table aside and start dancing. We'd dance and watch the sun rise over the bay. It would be six, seven o'clock in the morning. We had some wonderful, wonderful times."

There is another interesting island celebration which has been practiced here in Point Loma for many years, although it has also been somewhat modified. It is the *Festa da Madeira*, the Feast of Madeira. This originated in the Madeira Islands and is conducted there, as I understand it, on the Feast of Little Christmas. Here it is celebrated on Christmas Eve.

Around seven or eight o'clock at night on Christmas Eve, the people begin coming into the church in small groups, starting with the little children. Each group wears colorful costumes and is accompanied by musicians. The group marches up to the altar, singing. Before the crèche they leave their gifts, then they turn and go out. Other groups, older children, then youg adults, and so on, repeat the process. The last group consists of boys dressed as sailors, with a little replica of a fishing boat on wheels. It is about five feet long. They push it up to the crèche, heaped with gifts. By midnight the church is filled with people, the crèche and the boat are overflowing with gifts. In this atmosphere midnight mass is celebrated.

A few days later, the people have another get-together, with feasting and dancing. At that time, all the gifts are auctioned off, and the proceeds go to the church. The ceremony is held at Saint Agnes Church. I don't know any other church around this area which observes this ceremony.

The people from the island of Madeira are a group apart. They don't consider themselves attached to either the mainland Portuguese or the Azores Islanders. Madeira is part of an archipelago, 500 miles from Portugal, off the coast of Africa. It is the largest island. It was discovered in 1419 by João Goncalves Zarco and Tristão Vaz Teixeira. The people have their own customs, their own songs and their own celebrations, even on Christmas and New Years; yet we have had them come here on New Year's Eve to sing and visit and mingle with all the other Portuguese groups. We have considered this a great compliment, for they are a wonderful group of people and Madeira is a beautiful place.

The end of the year festivities held in Madeira are known all over the world. The people there have a legend which says

211

that God took pity on the people of the world after driving Adam and Eve out of the Garden of Eden; so He set aside Madeira, a small part of the original garden, for them.

Chapter XXV

The House That Lawrence Built

My wife and I have had a happy life together over the years and still do all right together. We think that this is because we talked things out right in the beginning, made decisions, and each one stuck to his word. We, also, always tried to treat each other with respect. We never wanted our children to hear us say harsh things to each other. My wife told me one day several years ago that our youngest son, Norman, came to her and said, "Mother I thought that every couple lived the way you and Dad do, but when I got out in the world, I got the surprise of my life. I found out that a lot of people don't live that way."

I think that most men must say, in all fairness, that if a marriage is happy, it is largely due to the wife. This is the way I feel, anyway. To be a good wife and a good mother is one of the hardest jobs in the world, but it's one of the most rewarding. I feel that maybe it was easier in our time because there was so much more family unity. Everybody had a place. There was always someone to turn to, who'd been through what you were going through. Everybody goes through the same experiences. My wife has remarked, "Most people seeing us in this big home today have the picture going through their minds that these people have got it made, that everything came easy, that we don't know what hardship is. It wasn't always this way for us. We had our differences, Lawrence and I. I was quite young when I married him, and I had always thought that Lawrence was just 'it.' I thought that he could do no wrong, but he always made us talk things out, and gradually I began to have my own opinions, which sometimes don't agree with his.

"We had problems. We had financial struggles and we had personal losses. Elaine, that was a sorrow, a year of anguish.

"Things worked out for us—maybe better than we deserved. We wound up with two fine sons and a fine daughter and nine wonderful grandchildren.

"Sometimes I think that we were more strict with our children after we made money than we had been before. One thing I always taught them was 'Look, you may have more than the next fellow, but don't ever let me see you looking down your nose at anybody. God has been very good to us. We have been fortunate, but that doesn't make you any better than anybody else. You must respect everyone—and because you have a little more, you also have a little more responsibility toward your fellow man.' Our children are raising their children in the same fashion in which we raised them. They are good men and women and good parents, and our grandchildren are a blessing to us.

"The grandchild who has the craziest hobby that I know of is Doris' boy, Drew. He loves reptiles. He's always got a snake, or an iguana, or a lizard, or polywogs or frogs, toads, Gila Monsters, you name it, and Drew has it. They all have names. He takes special interest in them. He can't get home from school fast enough to wind them around his arms to heat them.

"I get the 'heeby jeebies' every time we go to Rialto to visit, and in the middle of the night I start thinking that I am sleeping in a house where maybe a snake is loose. They have escaped from their cages. One little snake disappeared for two months. The odd thing is that they all come down the hall into Doris' room. She found that lost snake in a shoe when she went to put it on. She nearly fainted. She detests those things, but the child is so interested, what else can she do except to school herself? This is part of life, accepting people for what they are."

As with most people we have had bad days, but mainly we have happy memories, rewarding memories. Some events stand out. One year we gave a car to Mary's father for Christmas. The tree stood by the big bay window as usual. Mary handed

214

out the gifts from under it. The last gift she gave was to her father. It was a little card with a little toy automobile attached. He laughed when he saw it. Mary said, "Come on now, Dad, pick up that card, just pick it up." There was a ribbon tied to it. She had put the ribbon under the carpet all the way out the hall, up the stairway, and through the front door. In front of the house, tied with a bow was a car! He was pleased. He went around thanking everyone for the car.

Another time Mary had a seventy-fifth birthday party for him. People asked her, "What shall we bring for gifts?"

"Don't buy any gifts. If you want to, give him seventy-five pennies, fine, or seventy-five nickels, or seventy-five dimes, something like that."

We gave him seventy-five one dollar bills. Some people put their dimes in little baskets. Some put the money in great big boxes. They brought all kinds of odd packages. When he opened them and saw all the money, he exclaimed, "Oh, good, now I can pay my taxes."

Once he told Mary, "I've quit smoking."

"Oh, I don't believe it," she replied.

"Yes, I have."

"I'll give you a dime for every day you don't smoke."

"O.K., that's a go."

A whole year went by and he didn't smoke; so she gave him thirty-seven dollars. "I'm going downtown and buy me a suit," he declared. In those days you could buy a suit for that amount of money.

I remember the last dance he attended at the Portuguese Hall on Point Loma. It was festa time. He never missed those dances. We were having an open house. He came to the house and said, "Mary, I'm going to drink all that I feel like drinking and eat all that I want to eat. I'm going to dance until I'm ready to drop. I'm going to have a wonderful time today, because tomorrow I go to the doctor, and I have no idea what he is going to tell me."

The next day he went to the doctor. The following Sunday

was the last time he left his house. He had cancer. He lived for six months. He was bedridden during most of that period. We remembered and he remembered the wonderful time he had at his last festa. He talked about it often. Mary's mother lived seven years after he died. I could never forget them if I lived a thousand years. They were a part of our lives, a wonderful part of our lives.

Chapter XXVI

The Frosting On The Cake

When I sold the American Processing Company, in 1962, I announced that I was officially retired. I had been in business for myself for fifty years. I told my children that I was retiring, that it was up to them to carry on. Perhaps it's because I have said the same thing before that my wife and the children didn't seem to take my statements seriously. I had told them previously that I was "giving up the reins." They tell me that I have never done that yet—that I'm still "king of the castle." Maybe that's true. I do find it hard to let go. I love the challenge of work. I have always loved to work.

I disposed of the last of the tuna boats in 1970. Doris is running the golf course in Rialto and does a wonderful job; yet I worry. I keep in touch with her all the time. It's not that I don't have confidence in Doris. The course is always on my mind. I've got to know what's going on, how things are going, how we can improve.

I now keep an office in my home, with a secretary who comes in a few days a week. I still own my real estate in downtown San Diego, but I gave up my office there.

I keep up on politics, local and nation-wide. I have lived in this city for so long that I feel it is a part of me. I am interested in its future and in the future of our country. I have some definite opinions on these subjects. My wife knows that once a discussion of politics gets started in this house she had better start making the coffee.

Our home now is quiet most of the time. We don't entertain as much as we did. We don't go as much, but we keep up. Mary is happiest when the grandchildren and our children are here, or friends come, and she can cook and fuss over them. Our family celebrates birthdays and anniversaries and holidays together whenever possible. Mary said to Norman, one day recently, "It seems to me that we had such good times as a family years ago."

"Yes, and, Mother, we still do," he replied.

My aim now is to live as easy as I can, for as long as I can. I play golf some days, if I haven't anything pressing to do. I work in my yard. I water and cultivate around the vegetable garden and the flower beds. I like to monkey around. I like to see thing grows. I love to plant a seed and see it come up.

I have many fruit trees in my yard. One peach tree produces four kinds of grafted fruit. I have nectarines and plums, figs, loquats and tangerines, lemon trees and orange, guava, apricot, avocado—and flowers. I have all kinds of flowers. I've had gladiola plants that were over five feet tall. The Portuguese are known for their gardening ability, as well as being good fishermen. Back on the east coast they used to say that a potato wouldn't grow unless you spoke to it in Portuguese.

When I am in my yard, on the hillside overlooking the bay, I am reminded of my youth in Portugal, where I spent many days working in the warm sun and with a nice breeze blowing and the sea around me. Occasionally I look out over San Diego and see how it has grown since I first came here.

Some problems have come with age. I have bursitis in one of my hips and shoulders. My voice is not what it once was, yet I still love music and dancing. A few days ago we played some tapes of Portuguese songs here at the house. I couldn't help myself. I got up and danced Mary around the living room a few times—and this is a big living room.

I have some regrets. My wife says she once thought that I could do no wrong. I know better. I've made many mistakes. No one is more aware of them than I am. I made money, but not to be rich, which I'm not. I made it for others, for what I could do for others. I didn't make it fast enough to help some of those I should have helped—my father was one. Another was my uncle who first sent me to school in Chico. I couldn't help him while he lived—and he needed help. I helped his wife, though, I brought her to San Diego and built her a home on the back of our lot on Thirty-Second Street, a home for her and the grandniece whom she raised. I was the girl's godfather. I took care of them until the grandniece married, and they moved out.

Mary's uncle, who helped put me in business, died not too long ago. He was ninety years old. He lost his business in Oakland, and I asked him to come down here. I made a job for him in the plant. He and his wife, also, lived in the house we owned on Thirty-Second Street. I charged them enough to pay taxes, and after he passed on, I would have let her stay there, but she went into an apartment.

He once had a home in Oakland. I assisted him in saving that home. He paid me back. I helped him settle with his creditors when his business was in trouble. He paid me back for that, too. We turned to each other many times over the years. We were good friends.

I am a great believer in the Golden Rule. "Do unto others as you would have them do unto you." I wish that people all over the world would try to follow this precept. God knows we all need friends. I learned this from my own experiences. One thing I have always tried to remember is that in order to have friends you must be a friend. No matter how many modern inventions the world acquires, the need for friends persists.

I have never been able to turn a person away who asked for my assistance—even if it seemed his troubles were his own fault. Who am I to judge? I so often needed help myself and always got it from someone who didn't judge me. I've lost money lending it to people who never paid it back—never could pay it back—but that doesn't change my point of view.

Once in a while, too, you see something unusual develop from a situation where you lent a hand. This is very rewarding.

I remember one day in 1933, a man named Joe Viery, from Hayward, California, outside of Oakland, came to see me at my home. We had never met. He told me, "I know you only by reputation. I am broke. I need help."

That was during the depression. I was aware how bad the times were for many people. I gave Joe Viery a little money to tide him over until I found him a job. That was what he wanted—a job.

At that time, I owned a little shack on the waterfront. I had leased it out to an Armenian man who came to me and wanted to start a little restaurant there. This was at the foot of G Street. The place had no name. It was a little cubbyhole where people dropped in for a sandwich or a bowl of soup.

I understood that Joe Viery was a good cook and had worked in restaurants; so I went to the Armenian and asked him for a job for Joe, washing dishes and helping with the cooking.

He started working there. The next thing I knew, he had contracted with the owner to buy the restaurant, and he was leasing from me. He did very well. He operated there until 1935, then the city came and said it needed the site. I had been leasing the land from them. This would have put Joe out of business. I went to the city about this problem. The city fixed a place for me in the coal bunkers in the Spreckels Wharf. This was a larger and better place. When it was completed, and he moved in, he named it the Red Sails Inn.

He developed quite a restaurant business there, he and his wife. The place became very popular, a landmark of the city. It now is on Shelter Island. Later, he passed away, and his wife assumed the operation. The business continued to flourish. Eventually she sold it. One of the gifts I treasure is a menu and a complete dinner service from the Red Sails Inn.

I hope that the generations coming along will try to follow the Golden Rule more than it has been followed in the past. These young people have the responsibility for the future of the country. They are the best-educated group of people in our history. They ought to be able to comprehend the value of getting along. I hope so, anyway. I know that the use of this precept, plus my own personal belief in faith and love and determination, was of great aid to me in fulfilling my goals and handling my responsibilities.

For me, the goals and the responsibilities soon will terminate. I am aware of that, but as I said, it's hard to let go. I am concerned for the future of our country and the world. I'd still like to contribute. I suppose that this is one reason why I wanted to write a book on my life. I wanted it for my children and grandchildren; so that they would have a record of my life. I hope, though, that my story will be of help or encouragement to someone, sometime. I didn't write it solely to say what my material accomplishments have been. They, in themselves, don't make me a success and telling about them doesn't make this book a success. If the book shows that I have tried to be true to my beliefs and have at times been of some help to my fellow man, and if sometime it gives someone else a boost, then it and I will be a success.

People sometimes say to me, "What would you like to see your grandchildren become—doctors, or lawyers, or teachers?"

I tell these people that my wife and I have no desires for particular vocations for our grandchildren. These matters are their own decisions.

We do have some wishes for them. We want them to have all the education that they need and want. We want them to engage in a type of work which is honorable and gives them satisfaction. We want them to love their God and their country and their fellow man. If their lives are one-half as satisfactory as those of their grandparents, they will be fortunate people.

The one thing I would like to do most if I had my life to live over again would be to go to school—to go early enough that it would do me some good. I feel that an education would have helped me financially, socially, maybe to be a better husband and father and citizen—in every way.

It seems to me that I would have been able to use better judgment, learn better methods of work, things that I had to learn the hard way, by experimenting. Some of these things I have never learned, to this day.

Because of my limited schooling, I have always had a little inferiority complex. I'd be someplace, such as in a meeting, and I would have something which I wanted to say. I wouldn't know how to say it, how to explain what I meant, in order that people would understand. The words didn't come. I didn't have the background, the vocabulary.

Often I refused to speak in public, because I didn't feel myself competent. I also, turned down some positions of honor for this same reason. I would be aware of the fact that the others involved were much better educated than I was. I felt that I could not meet the demands of the occasion.

As I grow older, though, I find myself worrying less and less about my shortcomings. By now, everybody knows who I am and what I am.

For example, I did something the other night that I don't think I would have had the nerve to do a few years back. We went to a wedding at the Immaculata and to a dinner afterward. I knew the mother and the father of the bride very well—even the great-grandparents. Her grandfather was a close friend of mine.

The girl, a while back, was sick. She had some disease. Her parents were worried, and she was worried. Her mother told me about the problem outside the church one day. She was downcast; she was crying. The girl came up and kissed me. I saw that she, too, was tearful and worried. That sad child touched my heart. I told her, "Don't you worry. Be determined. Keep your faith in God. Say a few prayers. I will pray for you, also, and God will give you health."

She cheered up a bit. She kissed me again and left. Practically every time we met after that, she'd kiss me, and we'd talk. She'd say she hadn't given up. She still had faith and determination to be well.

She recovered her health. She became engaged. She was married a few days ago.

I kept thinking during that dinner, "By golly, I would like to get up and say something about this—and I'd like to sing a song to that girl."

The hall was full. There were three or four hundred people there. I knew all of the girl's people. She's Portuguese, but the boy was of Swedish descent. I didn't know any of the guests on his side. I thought, "Maybe I'd better not do anything. Maybe the words won't come—or the voice."

I kept thinking and thinking. During the dancing after the dinner, I passed the girl in the hall. She looked so happy, so different from the sick youngster that she had been, that I found myself saying, "Listen, nobody knows this but you and me. After the *Chamarita,* I am going to sing you a song for your wedding."

She smiled, "That's fine."

I went up to the musicians and asked , "Can you play 'Let Me Call You Sweetheart?' "

"We think so."

The guitarist sounded a note. I hummed it and said, "All right."

He told me, "Use this microphone," and he gave me a hand, pulling me up to the platform while everyone was dancing.

The drummer gave me a little introduction. The group became quiet. "Ladies and gentlemen," I remarked, "I've known this little girl ever since she was a tiny baby, and here a while back, she wasn't too well. I told her to keep faith and to pray for health, and that I would say some prayers for her. Tonight, I feel that the prayers of all who loved her and wanted her to be well have been heard. I want to sing her a song on her wedding night. I am the oldest person in this hall. I am past eighty-five, and my voice will probably crack when I get to the high tones; so don't be surprised."

The musicians started to play. I began to sing, "Let Me Call You Sweetheart." The groom was right down in front of me.

I sang a chorus, then asked everyone to join in with me. I don't know how many did. I couldn't see them or hear them, but Mary said, "It was quite a few and all young people. They gathered in a circle. Everyone else was amazed. They kept saying, 'Look at Lawrence with all the young people!' "

When I finished, everyone was crying. I didn't know whether it was because they were touched, or because my voice was so bad. I asked, "Did my voice crack much, Mary?"

She said, "It was beautifully done. Your voice was just right, like old times. You were the hit of the evening."

A man I know—he's a musician, he's Portuguese and he's played for me quite a few times—asked, "What got into you? I never heard you sing so well for years."

Another man, a friend of the groom's family, came up. I didn't even know him. We shook hands. "It was a beautiful wedding," I remarked.

He replied, "You sure put the frosting on the cake!"

INDEX